Yoga Tantra
Paths to Magical Feats

Yoga Tantra

Paths to Magical Feats

His Holiness the Dalai Lama
Dzong-ka-ba
Jeffrey Hopkins

Translated and edited by Jeffrey Hopkins

Co-edited by Kevin A. Vose and Steven N. Weinberger

Snow Lion Publications
Ithaca, New York
Boulder, Colorado

Snow Lion Publications
605 West State Street
P. O. Box 6483
Ithaca, New York 14851 USA
(607) 273-8519
www.snowlionpub.com

First edition USA 2005

Printed in USA on acid-free, recycled paper.

ISBN 1-55939-237-1
ISBN 978-1-55939-237-2

Library of Congress Cataloging-in-Publication Data
Yoga Tantra : paths to magical feats / Dalai Lama, Dzong-ka-ba ; translated, edited, and annotated by Jeffrey Hopkins ; co-edited by Kevin A. Vose and Steven N. Weinberger. -- 1st ed.
p. cm.
Includes English translation of the fourth section of Rgyal ba khyab bdag rdo rje 'chaṅ chen po'i lam gyi rim pa gsaṅ ba kun gyi gnad rnam par phye ba.
Includes bibliographical references.
ISBN-13: 978-1-55939-237-2 (alk. paper)
ISBN-10: 1-55939-237-1 (alk. paper)
1. Yoga (Tantric Buddhism) 2. Spiritual life--Tantric Buddhism. 3. Buddhism--China--Tibet--Doctrines.
I. Bstan-'dzin-rgya-mtsho, Dalai Lama XIV, 1935- . II. Hopkins, Jeffrey. III. Tsoṅ-kha-pa Blo-bzaṅ-grags-pa, 1357-1419. Rgyal ba khyab bdag rdo rje 'chaṅ chen po'i lam gyi rim pa gsaṅ ba kun gyi gnad rnam par phye ba. English. Selections.
BQ7805. Y65 2005
294.3'4436--dc22

2005012799

Contents

Detailed Outline

III: *Supplement*
by Ke-drup-ge-lek-b̄el-sang 121

List of Charts

List of Illustrations

demonstrated by Jhado Tulku, abbot emeritus of Namgyel Tantric College (see insert)

Preface
by Jeffrey Hopkins

This book on Yoga Tantra is the third in a series presenting *The Stages of the Path to a Conqueror and Pervasive Master, a Great Vajradhara: Revealing All Secret Topics*[a] by the late-fourteenth- and early-fifteenth-century scholar and yogi Ḏzong-ka-ḇa Ḻo-sang-drak-ḇa[b] of Tibet. By way of introducing the present book, let us briefly consider Ḏzong-ka-ḇa's procedure in the first two volumes.

1. TANTRA IN TIBET

Ḏzong-ka-ḇa's text begins the *Great Exposition of Secret Mantra,*[c] as it is also called, with an examination of the difference between the Buddhist vehicles. That section—presented in the first book in this series, *Tantra in Tibet*[1]—mainly analyzes a variety of earlier delineations of the difference between the Sūtra Great Vehicle and the Mantra Great Vehicle. Although he does not mention Bu-d̄ön Rin-chen-drup[d] (1290-1364) by name, it is apparent that his prime source is Bu-d̄ön's encyclopedic presentation of the difference between Sūtra and Mantra in his *Extensive General Presentation of the Tantra Sets, Key Opening the Door to the Precious Treasury of Tantra Sets.*[e] Bu-d̄ön lists presentations by several Indian scholars who delineate various numbers of ways the Mantra Great Vehicle surpasses the Sūtra Great Vehicle, or Perfection Vehicle as it is commonly called:

---

[a] *rgyal ba khyab bdag rdo rje 'chang chen po'i lam gyi rim pa gsang ba kun gyi gnad rnam par phye ba;* completed in 1404.

[b] *tsong kha pa blo bzang grags pa;* 1357-1419.

[c] *sngags rim chen mo.*

[d] *bu ston rin chen grub.*

[e] *rgyud sde spyi'i rnam par gzhag pa: rgyud sde rin po che'i mdzes rgyan,* Collected Works, (New Delhi: International Academy of Indian Culture, 1969), vol. 15, 6.1-32.5. The very same presentation, with minor printing differences, is repeated in Bu-d̄ön's middle length version called the *Medium Length General Presentation of the Tantra Sets: Illuminating the Secrets of All Tantra Sets* (*rgyud sde spyi'i rnam par gzhag pa rgyud sde thams cad kyi gsang ba gsal bar byed pa*), vol. 15, 614.7-641.7. A considerably abbreviated version of the same is given in his *Condensed General Presentation of the Tantra Sets: Key Opening the Door to the Precious Treasury of Tantra Sets* (*rgyud sde spyi'i rnam par gzhag pa rgyud sde rin po che'i gter sgo 'byed pa'i lde mig*), vol. 14, 845.1-859.1.

- Tripiṭakamāla and commentator Vajrapāṇi—four differences
- Jñānashrī—eleven differences
- Ratnākarashānti—three differences
- Nāgārjuna—six differences[a]
- Indrabhuti—seven differences
- Jñānapāda—three differences
- Ḍombhiheruka—five differences
- Vajraghaṇṭapāda—four differences
- Samayavajra—five differences.

In a radical departure from Bu-d̄ön's catalogue of opinions, D̄zong-ka-b̄a analyzes the structure of the path to Buddhahood and analytically chooses to emphasize a single central distinctive feature of the Mantra Vehicle, deity yoga. The main points he makes in distinguishing the Lesser Vehicle and the Great Vehicle and, within the latter, the Sūtra and Mantra forms, are:

- The difference between vehicles must lie in the sense of "vehicle" as that to which one progresses or as that by which one progresses.
- The Lesser Vehicle differs from the Great Vehicle in both. The destination of the lower one is the state of a Hearer or Solitary Realizer Foe Destroyer and of the higher one, Buddhahood.
- Concerning "vehicle" in the sense of means by which one progresses, although there is no difference in the wisdom realizing emptiness, there is a difference in method—Lesser Vehicle not having and Great Vehicle having the altruistic intention to become enlightened and its attendant deeds.
- Sūtra and Mantra Great Vehicle do not differ in terms of the goal, the state being sought, since both seek the highest enlightenment of a Buddha, but there is a difference in the means of progress, again not in wisdom but in method.
- Within method, Sūtra and Mantra Great Vehicle differ not in the basis or motivation, the altruistic intention to become enlightened, nor in having the perfections as deeds, but in the additional technique of deity yoga. A deity is a supramundane being who himself or herself is a manifestation of compassion and wisdom. Thus, in the special practice of deity yoga one joins one's own body, speech, mind, and activities with

---

[a] Bu-d̄ön's source for this and the remaining presentations is Atisha's *Compilation of All Pledges* (*dam tshig thams cad bsdus pa, sarvasamayasaṃgraha*); Peking 4547, vol. 81. Thanks to Kevin Vose for this note.

> the exalted body, speech, mind, and activities of a supramundane being, manifesting on the path a similitude of the state of the effect.

As scriptural authority for the central distinguishing feature between the Sūtra and Mantra Great Vehicles, D̄zong-ka-b̄a quotes a passage from the *Vajrapañjara Tantra*,[a] rejects the commentaries of Kṛṣhṇapāda and Indrabodhi,[b] and critically uses the commentary of Devakulamahāmati,[2] accepting some parts and rejecting others. He reinforces his presentation of deity yoga as the dividing line between the two Great Vehicles with citations from or references to works on Highest Yoga Tantra by Jñānapāda,[3] Ratnākarashānti,[4] Abhayākāra,[5] Durjayachandra,[6] Shrīdhara,[7] Samayavajra,[8] Jinadatta,[9] and Vinayadatta.[10]

Despite D̄zong-ka-b̄a's many citations of tantras and Indian commentaries, it is clear that they are used only as supportive evidence for his argument. Tradition is only supportive, not the ultimate authority. The arbiter is reason, specifically in the sense of determining coherence and consistency within a path structure. D̄zong-ka-b̄a refutes Ratnarakṣhita and Tripiṭakamāla,[11] for instance, not because they differ from the aforementioned sources but because their presentations fail in terms of consistency with the path structure. By doing so, he moves the basis of the presentation from scriptural citation to reasoned analysis of a meditative structure.

Also, whereas Bu-d̄ön catalogues nine ways that Indian scholar-yogis differentiate the four tantra sets—by way of the four Indian castes, four schools of tenets, four faces of Kālachakra, four periods of the day, four eras, followers of four deities, four afflictive emotions to be abandoned, four levels of desire to be purified, and four levels of faculties—D̄zong-ka-b̄a critically examines most of these, accepting only the last two, with modification. He differentiates the four Tantra sets by way of their main trainees being of four very different types, since these trainees have (1) four different ways of using desire for the attributes of the Desire Realm in the path and (2) four different levels of capacity for generating the emptiness and deity yogas that use desire in the path.

---

[a] *mkha' 'gro ma rdo rje gur shes bya ba'i rgyud kyi rgyal po chen po'i brtag pa, dākinī-vajrapañjara-mahātantrarāja-kalpa;* Peking 11, vol. 1. See *Tantra in Tibet,* 117.

[b] *Tantra in Tibet,* 120. Kṛṣhṇapāda's commentary is *mkha' 'gro ma rdo rje gur shes bya ba'i rgyud kyi rgyal po chen po'i brtag pa'i rgyal po'i bshad sbyar, ḍākinīvajrapañjaranāma-mahātantrarājakalpamukhabandha;* Peking 2325, vol. 54. Indrabodhi's commentary is *mkha' 'gro ma rdo rje gur gyi dka' 'grel shal nas brgyud pa, ḍākinīvajrapañjaramahātantrarājasya-pañjikāprathamapaṭalamukhabandha;* Peking 2324, vol. 54.

In his systemization, the four tantras are not differentiated (1) by way of their *object of intent* since all four are aimed at bringing about others' welfare, or (2) by way of the *object of attainment* they are seeking since all four seek the full enlightenment of Buddhahood, or (3) by way of merely having different types of *deity yoga* since all four tantra sets have many different types of deity yoga but are each only one tantra set. Rather, the distinctive tantric practice of deity yoga, motivated by great compassion and beginning with emptiness yoga, is carried out in different ways in the four tantra sets. Various levels of desire—involved in gazing, smiling, touching, and sexual union—are utilized by the respective main trainees in accordance with their disposition toward styles of practice, these being to emphasize external activities, to balance external activities and meditative stabilization, to emphasize meditative stabilization, or to exclusively focus on meditative stabilization.

D̄zong-ka-b̄a's exposition represents an appeal to analysis, a carefully constructed argument based on scriptural sources and reasoning, with the emphasis on the latter. Consistency, coherence, and elegance of system are the cornerstones; his procedure is that of a thorough scholar, analyzing sources and counter-opinions with careful scrutiny and determining the place of the pillars of his analysis in the general structure of a system. His intention is clearly not to present a catalogue of views as Bu-d̄ön mainly does, but to adjudicate conflicting systems of interpretation, thereby establishing a radically new one.

2. *DEITY YOGA*

The second and third sections of the *Great Exposition of Secret Mantra*, concerned with Action Tantra and Performance Tantra, are presented in the second book in this series, *Deity Yoga*.[12] At the start of his exposition of Action Tantra, D̄zong-ka-b̄a critically examines an issue that Bu-d̄ön left hanging: Does Action Tantra have imagination of oneself as a deity or only imagination of a deity in front of oneself? Bu-d̄ön[13] catalogues conflicting opinions on the topic, and after presenting a detailed case against reasons behind Buddhaguhya's and Varabodhi's assertion that Action Tantras involve imagination of oneself as a deity, leaves the issue with advice to analyze which side is right. However, in explaining the path procedure of Action Tantra,[14] Bu-d̄ön presents the system of those who say it has deity yoga. The apparent self-contradiction is explained by the encyclopedic nature of his work, built on an intention to include as many systems and viewpoints as possible.

Reacting to Bu-dön's presentation, Dzong-ka-ba argues the case that even though deity yoga is absent from most Action Tantras, it is required for the main trainees of Action Tantra. He examines at length Indian commentarial sources for the opposite view in the assertions of three Indian scholars—Shrīdhara, Jinadatta, and Indrabhuti—and, on the basis of the favored opinion of two Indian Action Tantra commentators, Buddhaguhya and Varabodhi, who hold that deity yoga (here meaning imagination of oneself as a deity) is essential to the mode of procedure in Action Tantra, explains away an apparently contradictory statement in a tantra, the *Wisdom Vajra Compendium.*[15] Dzong-ka-ba, living within the richness of tradition provided by Bu-dön, had the opportunity to sift through these traditions to creatively find an elegant, internally consistent system; Bu-dön's catalogue most likely made this possible.

Dzong-ka-ba then lays out the procedure of practice in Action Tantra, mainly combining the expositions in two tantras—the *Susiddhi Tantra*[a] and the *Concentration Continuation Tantra*[b]—and their respective expositions by Varabodhi[c] and Buddhaguhya.[d] The *Concentration Continuation* and Buddhaguhya's commentary present the actual meditations clearly but do not detail the preliminary rites, the pledges, and so forth, which Dzong-ka-ba takes from the *Susiddhi* and Varabodhi's formulation of it into a practice rite called a Means of Achievement.[e] Almost all of Dzong-ka-ba's presentation can be found in these four texts; his creative innovation is to interweave them into a complete system of practice of this class of tantra.

Dzong-ka-ba's brief exposition of Performance Tantra, on the other hand, is drawn only from the *Vairochanābhisambodhi Tantra* and Buddhaguhya's *Condensation*[16] of it, aimed at affording a glimpse into its yogic procedure.

---

a *legs grub kyi rgyud, susiddhitantra;* P431, vol. 9.

b *bsam gtan phyi ma rim par phye pa, dhyānottarapaṭalakrama;* P430, vol. 9.

c In Tibetan, his name is usually *byang chub mchog,* but Dül-dzin-drak-ba-gyel-tsen gives it as *ye shes mchog.* His commentary is *legs par grub par byed pa'i sgrub pa'i thabs bsdus pa, susiddhikarasādhanasaṃgraha;* P3890, vol. 79.

d *sangs rgyas gsang ba.* His commentary is *bsam gtan phyi ma rim par phye ba rgya cher bshad pa, dhyānottarapaṭalaṭīkā;* P3495, vol. 78.

e *sgrub thabs, sādhana.*

3. *YOGA TANTRA: PATHS AND FEATS*

In the section on Yoga Tantra, presented here in this third book, Ḏzong-ka-ḇa compares explanations of the *Compendium of Principles Tantra*[17] (the root Yoga Tantra) and of the *Vajrashekhara Tantra*[18] (the primary explanatory tantra)[a] by the Indian scholars Buddhaguhya, Ānandagarbha, and Shākyamitra—known as "the three masters expert in Yoga Tantra." By interweaving portions of their expositions he creates a new exposition.

Ḏzong-ka-ḇa cites Buddhaguhya and Ānandagarbha each about thirty times and Shākyamitra about ten times. The texts are:

Buddhaguhya
- *Introduction to the Meaning of the Tantra*[19]

Ānandagarbha
- *Illumination of the Principles*[20]
- longer and shorter *Means of Achievement Called "Source of Vajrasattva"*[21]
- *Rite of the Vajra Element Great Maṇḍala: Source of All Vajras*[22]
- *Extensive Explanation of the "Shrīparamādya Tantra"*[23]

Shākyamitra
- *Ornament of Kosala*[24]

Ḏzong-ka-ḇa cites Buddhaguhya's *Introduction to the Meaning of the Tantra* and Ānandagarbha's several works throughout the sections on the yogas with and without signs and on the techniques for achieving special yogic feats. However, his several citations of Shākyamitra's *Ornament of Kosala* are found only with respect to the concentrated meditative state called calm abiding and with respect to the nature of special insight.

About these Indian masters, Steven Weinberger says:[b]

> The earliest of the "three people expert in Yoga Tantra" (*yo ga la mi mkhas pa gsum*), as Tibetan traditions refer to them, Buddhaguhya was an influential figure in the early propagation of Buddhism in Tibet during the height of its dynastic period. While in western

---

[a] He also cites a few times the *Shrīparamādya Tantra* (*dpal mchog dang po, śrīparamādya;* P120, vol. 5; Toh. 488, vol. *ta,* 228a.3), which is another explanatory tantra.

[b] Steven Weinberger, *The Significance of Yoga Tantra and the* Compendium of Principles (Tattvasaṃgraha) *within Tantric Buddhism in India and Tibet* (Ann Arbor: University Microfilms, 2003), 85-88. See Weinberger's work for much valuable detail on the history and nature of Yoga Tantra.

Tibet in the environs of Mt. Kailash, he was invited to central Tibet by Trisong Detsen and, although he declined the invitation, sent several of his commentaries (reportedly composed for this purpose). In addition, he is also an important figure in the Mahāyoga tradition preserved by the Nyingma School in Tibet...

The dates for Śākyamitra and Ānandagarbha are less certain. Śākyamitra probably lived during the latter half of the eighth century (and perhaps into the first half of the ninth century). Of the three, he authored the fewest extant texts. However, his exegesis of the *Compendium of Principles*—the *Kosala Ornament: Extensive Explanation of the "Compendium of Principles"*—is a seminal Yoga Tantra work. While Buddhaguhya's *Entry into the Meaning of the Tantra* is earlier, it is an explanation of important doctrines and practices of the *Compendium of Principles* (it is sometimes referred to in Tibetan traditions as esoteric instructions [*man ngag*] for the tantra). Śākyamitra's *Kosala Ornament*, although written after Buddhaguhya's work, represents the first word-by-word commentary on the *Compendium of Principles*, and as such is a seminal exegesis.

Ānandagarbha, the latest of "three people expert in Yoga Tantra," can tentatively be dated to the latter part of the ninth or early part of the tenth century. A Tibetan source that dates him to an earlier period is Tāranātha's early seventeenth-century work *History of Buddhism in India*, which states that Ānandagarbha lived during the reign of King Mahīpāla, who died at roughly the same time as the Tibetan King Relpacen (d. 838 or 841). This would put Ānandagarbha sometime during the late eighth or early ninth century.

However, I think this account is in error. Butön says that Ānandagarbha and Mañjuśrīkīrti were "spiritual brothers" (*mched grogs*), which means they would have been contemporaries, and Ronald Davidson dates Mañjuśrīkīrti to the tenth century. Thus, if Mañjuśrīkīrti and Ānandagarbha were indeed contemporaries, then Ānandagarbha must have been alive during the tenth century. This assessment seems probable, given the range of tantras on which Ānandagarbha composed commentaries, some of which represented later developments of Indian Buddhist tantra. He is taken in Tibetan traditions to be the authoritative Indian Yoga Tantra author, and this is due at least in part to the fact that he represents later

> developments of the tradition—certainly later than Buddhaguhya and Śākyamitra. Thus, I locate Ānandagarbha toward the end of the ninth or beginning of the tenth century.
>
> There is some biographical information on Ānandagarbha preserved in Tibetan sources. He was a native of Magadha and a resident of Vikramaśīla monastery. A prolific tantric exegete, his corpus of works includes commentaries and liturgical texts on a range of tantras. He wrote an enormous commentary on the *Compendium of Principles* known by its abbreviated title *Illumination of the Principles.* He also composed a maṇḍala rite for the Vajradhātu Great Maṇḍala—the central maṇḍala of the *Compendium of Principles* and of the Yoga Tantra class as a whole. In addition, he composed a maṇḍala rite for the Conquest over the Three Worlds Maṇḍala, the first maṇḍala of the second section of the *Compendium of Principles.*
>
> Ānandagarbha also authored a number of texts on other Yoga Tantras. He wrote a commentary on and a maṇḍala rite for the *Śrī Paramādya Tantra.* In addition, he wrote commentaries and ritual texts for the *Purification of All Bad Transmigrations* as well as consecration rites and texts for the practice of deities such as Vajrasattva. He also authored exegetical works on the *Secret Assembly (Guhyasamāja) Tantra* and the *Magical Emanation Net (Māyājāla) Tantra.*

Though much of Dzong-ka-ba's explanation is drawn from the extensive works on Yoga Tantra by Bu-dön,[a] it is clear that he consulted the treatises by these three Indian scholars and wove a new presentation. Nevertheless, neither he nor his chief disciples wrote at length on Yoga Tantra, likely from high estimation of Bu-dön's scholarship on the topic.

Introduction, Exposition, and Supplement

Dzong-ka-ba's presentation of Yoga Tantra is introduced by His Holiness the Fourteenth Dalai Lama, Tenzin Gyatso, in the first part of this book. This introduction is drawn mainly from his lectures on Dzong-ka-ba's text given in Dharmsala, India, in 1979, but also from lectures given in the summer of 2002 and from private discussions.[b]

---

a See the Bibliography.

b The Dalai Lama's commentaries included in the first two books in this series were translated and edited from private teachings in Dharmsala in 1974.

Ḏzong-ka-ḇa's exposition of Yoga Tantra comprises the second part of this book. The third part is a supplement on the central practices of the five manifest enlightenments and the four seals, written by Ḏzong-ka-ḇa's student Ke-drup-ge-lek-ḇel-sang. The fourth and final part is my brief formulation of the steps of Yoga Tantra practice, drawn from the Dalai Lama's, Ḏzong-ka-ḇa's, and Ke-drup-ge-lek-ḇel-sang's explanations. The First Paṇchen Lama Ḻo-sang-chö-ḡyi-gyel-tsen's[a] depiction of the five manifest enlightenments is given in an Appendix.

I wish to acknowledge teachings from the late Jam-ḇel-shen-pen,[b] abbot emeritus of the Lower Tantric College in Hunsa, India, in June, 1980, on Ḏzong-ka-ḇa's presentation of Yoga Tantra at UMA in Boonesville, Virginia, as well as assistance from Lati Rin-ḇo-chay, abbot emeritus of Shartse College in Mundgod, Karnataka, India; Ḏen-ḇa-ḏen-dzin, abbot emeritus of Gomang College of Dre-ḇung Monastic University in Mundgod, Karnataka, India; and Jhado Tulku, abbot emeritus of Namgyel Tantric College in Dharmsala, India, who taught me the outline of a Yoga Tantra practice text and provided the hand-configurations that I photographed and have included here. I deeply appreciate input from Dr. Steven N. Weinberger, whose expertise gained from writing his doctoral thesis on Yoga Tantra proved invaluable in bringing this book to a conclusion, as well as Kevin A. Vose's wide-ranging assistance throughout the manuscript.

Jeffrey Hopkins
University of Virginia

---

a *blo bzang chos kyi rgyal mtshan,* 1567[?]-1662.

b He subsequently became the Throne-Holder of Ganden, head of the Ge-luk-ḇa order.

I: The Features of Yoga Tantra

by His Holiness the Dalai Lama

1. The Basics

To succeed in practicing any form of tantra, it is necessary first to train in developing the altruistic intention to become enlightened. Ḏzong-ka-ḇa says that this needs to be done "in accordance with the quintessential instructions," these being found in his *Great Exposition of the Stages of the Path to Enlightenment*.[a] Specifically, such an altruistic intention is generated by way of the seven cause and effect quintessential instructions or the equalizing and switching of self and other. To do those, it is necessary to identify what liberation is and to develop an awareness seeking liberation, for which it is necessary to reflect on the three types of suffering and develop an intention to turn away from over-emphasizing the appearances of this life and then to turn away from over-emphasizing the appearances of future lives, developing an intention to leave such cyclic existence entirely, whereupon it is possible to reflect on how others suffer and develop compassion. Done continuously over a long period of time, at best one should develop a fully qualified altruistic intention to become enlightened, and at least one should develop such an intention from the depths of the heart.

With such altruism as your basic motivation it is possible to receive initiation and take the pledges that lay out a type of behavior conducive to enlightenment. Sometimes people mistakenly look on vows and pledges as if these were a type of punishment, but this is not at all the case. For example, just as we follow certain methods of eating and drinking to improve our health and certainly not to punish ourselves, so the rules that Shākyamuni Buddha formulated are for controlling counter-productive ill-deeds and ultimately for overcoming afflictive emotions, because these are self-ruinous. Thus, to relieve oneself from suffering, one controls the motivations and deeds producing suffering for one's own sake. Realizing from his own experience that suffering stems from one's own afflictive emotions as well as actions contaminated with them, he set forth styles of behavior to reduce the problem for our own profit, certainly not to give us a hard time. Hence, these rules are for the sake of controlling sources of harm.

Otherwise, it seems that nowadays some people look on the practice of religion as if it were something that causes them to lose their freedom. Opposite to this, these rules are for the sake of utilizing your freedom to de-

[a] See Tsong-kha-pa, *The Great Treatise on the Stages of the Path to Enlightenment*, 3 vols., ed. Joshua W. C. Cutler and Guy Newland (Ithaca, N.Y.: Snow Lion, 2000-2004).

velop the limitless qualities of Buddhahood, in the quest for which you should never be satisfied. Toward material things, which necessarily have a limit, it is best to be satisfied with what you have, but with regard to the limitless development of spiritual qualities, you should never be satisfied with a mere portion, but continually seek higher development. The rules themselves make your mind conducive to such progress, so there is no reason to be uptight about them.

YOGA TANTRA

All four classes of Buddhist tantra involve the practice of deity yoga in which the wisdom realizing emptiness appears itself as an ideal, compassionately effective being. Those that, when performing deity yoga, put particular emphasis on external activities such as bathing are Action Tantras. Those that put equal emphasis on performing external activities and internal yoga are Performance Tantras. Those that, between external activities and internal yoga, put particular emphasis on internal yoga are Yoga Tantras—our topic here.

What is yoga? In general, yoga (*rnal 'byor*) is the joining (*'byor*) of the mind to a natural, pristine, actual (*rnal*) meaning.[a] This mainly is the undifferentiable joining of method and wisdom, which is identified as the undifferentiable joining of the mind of enlightenment and the perfection of wisdom realizing emptiness. Here it seems that the "mind of enlightenment" is not only the altruistic intention to become enlightened; rather, since the altruistic intention to become enlightened aims at enlightenment, and specifically Form Bodies, in order to be of service to others, the object of observation includes Form Bodies, and thus divine body—the body of a deity—within the exalted mind and exalted body of Buddhahood, and thus "method" comes to indicate deity yoga. Thereby, "yoga" here refers to the union of deity yoga and the wisdom realizing emptiness. Tantras, in general, teach such a yoga of the undifferentiability of method and wisdom.

Among texts teaching such a union, some mainly teach method, whereas others mainly teach wisdom, due to which Bu-dön Rin-chen-drup[b] says that Yoga Tantras are divided into two types—method, or father, tantras and wisdom, or mother, tantras. The root Yoga Tantra, the *Compendium of Principles Tantra,* mainly teaches the ten principles of Yoga Tantra

---

a *don rnal ma la 'byor ba.*

b *bu ston rin chen grub;* 1290-1364.

and thus is a father, or method, tantra; the ten principles are:

1. maṇḍala[a]
2. mantra[b]
3. seal[c]
4. self-protection and place protection[d]
5. rite of invitation[e]
6. repetition[f]
7. meditation[g]
8. external and internal burnt offering[h]
9. withdrawal[i]
10. having made offering, requesting departure.[j]

The *Shrīparamādya Tantra,*[25] on the other hand, emphasizes the teaching of wisdom, due to which it is a mother, or wisdom, tantra.

The term "tantra" means continuum; as the *Guhyasamāja Tantra* says:[k]

> Tantra is renowned as "continuum."
> It is asserted as of three aspects.

The explanatory tantra of the *Compendium of Principles Tantra*[26] called the *Vajrashekhara*[27] says that:

- the basic tantra[l] refers to sentient beings, since all have the matrix-of-One-Gone-Thus
- the fruit tantra[m] is Buddhahood itself

---

a *dkyil 'khor.*

b *sngags.*

c *phyag rgya.*

d *bdag dang gnas srung ba.*

e *spyan drang pa'i cho ga.*

f *bzlas brjod.*

g *sgom pa.*

h *phyi nang gi bdag nyid can kyi sbyin sregs.*

i *nye bar 'du ba;* a gathering back of the deities that you emanated.

j *mchod nas gzhegs su gsol ba;* as the final step in the process, requesting the deities to depart after you have gathered them back and made offerings to them.

k P81, vol. 3, 200.1.2: *rgyud ni rgyun zhes bya ba grags/ de ni rnam pa gsum du 'dod.*

l *gzhi'i rgyud.*

m *'bras bu'i rgyud.*

- the continuation-tantra[a] is the means by which you pass beyond or cross over cyclic existence—a guru.

In another way, the *Vajrashekhara Tantra* says that the "continuation-tantra" is nirvāṇa, and "tantra" is cyclic existence. The meaning here is that the single continuum of our basic constituent, the matrix-of-One-Gone-to-Bliss, luminous and cognitive mind, while together with the defilements of afflictive emotions, is cyclic existence, and when defilements have been utterly abandoned and one is endowed with the good qualities of having so separated, is nirvāṇa. Thus, tantra has the sense of being included within the continuum of consciousness, or within the continuum of a sentient being, in terms of which cyclic existence and nirvāṇa are posited.

A continuum of words that are a means of expression (a word-tantra) that takes this meaning-continuum as its topic of expression is designated with the name "Tantra." With respect to Yoga Tantras that are means of expression, one needs to know how the Teacher Buddha initially set them forth and the history of their exposition in India and in Tibet, for which you should consult the works of Bu-d̄ön;[b] D̄zong-ka-b̄a does not treat these topics.

THE ROOT TANTRA

In the root Yoga Tantra, the *Compendium of Principles,* the introduction teaches about the state of Vairochana endowed with the fulfillment of your own and other's aims, thereby engendering a wish in listeners to attain this. For instance, Maitreya's description of an exalted-knower-of-all-aspects [that is, an omniscient consciousness] in the first chapter of his *Ornament for Clear Realization*[28] has the purpose of causing trainees who see these qualities to wish to attain them and make exertion to do so. In the same way, the description—in the introduction to the *Compendium of Principles Tantra*—of the state of a Vairochana who is endowed with the fulfillment of both your own and others' aims engenders a wish to attain the qualities of this fruitional state. The tantra then sets forth the means to attain this

---

[a] *rgyud phyi ma, uttaratantra.*

[b] Specifically, Bu-d̄ön's *Ship for Launching onto the Ocean of Yoga Tantra* (*rnal 'byor rgyud kyi rgya mtshor 'jug pa'i gru gzings,* in Collected Works of Bu ston, Part 11 *da* [Lhasa: Zhol Printing House, 1990; photographic reproduction Delhi: International Academy of Indian Culture, 1968), 1a.1-92b.2]. For material drawn from this text, see Weinberger, *The Significance of Yoga Tantra,* especially Chapter Two.

state—mundane feats,[a] such as pacification of illness, and supramundane feats, the final parinirvāṇa as well as, perhaps, the path of seeing and so forth.

The first of the four sections of the *Compendium of Principles Tantra,* called the "Vajra Element,"[b] is associated with the Vairochana lineage and thus exalted body. Its being first indicates that, as in Highest Yoga Tantra, body is chief. The second section, "Conquest over the Three Realms,"[c] is associated with Akṣhobhya and the vajra lineage—exalted mind. The third section, "Taming Transmigrators,"[d] is associated with Amitābha and the lotus lineage—exalted speech. The fourth section, "Achieving Aims,"[e] is associated with Ratnasambhava and the jewel lineage—exalted activities in terms of their agent. When this last lineage is taken from the viewpoint not of the agent but of the activity, it is associated with Amoghasiddhi and the action lineage. Thus, there are four sections and five lineages.

The *Vajrashekhara,* an explanatory tantra, says:

> Because the lineages have many aspects,
> The lineages are said to be a hundred;
> In brief there are five aspects.

Thus, in brief there are five lineages, which can, in turn, be divided into twenty-five:

- the Vairochana lineage of the Vairochana lineage
- the Akṣhobhya lineage of the Vairochana lineage
- the Amitābha lineage of the Vairochana lineage
- the Ratnasambhava lineage of the Vairochana lineage
- the Amoghasiddhi lineage of the Vairochana lineage

and so on with respect to the other four lineages. These, in turn, are divided into four each in terms of [four types of mantra:] essence, seal, secret-mantra, and knowledge-mantra, making one hundred lineages. They are all contained in the five lineages—Vairochana, Akṣhobhya, Amitābha, Ratnasambhava, and Amoghasiddhi, or, as they are also called, Buddha [or One-Gone-Thus], vajra, doctrine [or lotus], jewel, and action lineages. When

---

[a] *dngos grub, siddhi;* actual yogic accomplishments.

[b] *rdo rje dbyings, vajradhātu.*

[c] *'jig rten gsum rgyal, trilokavijaya.*

[d] *'gro 'dul, sakalajagadvinaya.*

[e] *don grub, sarvārthasiddhi.*

these five are set forth in the four sections of the *Compendium of Principles Tantra,* the last two lineages are treated as one.

The *Compendium of Principles* has supplemental divisions. The one called the "Continuation of the *Compendium of Principles Tantra*" is taught for the supreme of trainees. Another, called the "Continuation of the Continuation of the *Compendium of Principles Tantra*" is taught for those of lesser faculties and thus mainly contains external rites. Both of these describe paths for all four lineages. Since the "Continuation of the Continuation" was spoken for those who cannot perform deity yoga but who achieve feats mainly in dependence on rites using external substances, repetition of mantra, and so forth, it might seem to contradict the explanation that Yoga Tantras were taught for trainees who mainly emphasize meditation. However, it is not contradictory because, although the chief trainees for whom the Yoga Tantras were spoken are those involved mainly in the yoga of the union of the profound and the manifest and capable of cultivating the entire spectrum of paths, there are also secondary trainees who need not be of this type.

The four sections of the *Compendium of Principles Tantra* are, from one viewpoint, for different persons, but from another viewpoint all four sections are to be used by a single practitioner of any lineage. In the sense that the individual sections were taught for the sake of persons with different dispositions, they are mainly for individuals of four different lineages, or types. Since a mantra-repeater, or practitioner, of the One-Gone-Thus lineage has—from among the afflictive emotions of desire, hatred, obscuration, and miserliness—a predominance of desire, the section that teaches the paths of the One-Gone-Thus lineage, called the "Vajra Element," describes maṇḍalas in which the deities have an aspect slightly desirous. Similarly, since a practitioner of the vajra lineage has, in terms of the afflictive emotions, a predominance of hatred, the second section, "Conquest over the Three Realms," depicts maṇḍalas with slightly fierce deities as the lords, such as Akṣhobhya and Huṃkara. Practitioners of the lotus lineage have a greater tendency towards obscuration and wrong views than the other afflictive emotions, due to which the third section, "Taming Transmigrators," depicts deities in a variety of aspects. Practitioners of the jewel lineage have a greater tendency towards miserliness, due to which the fourth section, "Achieving Aims," speaks of deities with a slightly more expansive and magnificent bearing. Thus, from this viewpoint, the four sections are intended for four separate types of persons who differ in terms of thought, disposition, and potential. This is similar to the Highest Yoga Tantra teaching that desirous persons can gain achievement more easily if they rely on Amitābha, whereas persons who tend toward hatred can gain achievement more easily in dependence on Akṣhobhya, and so forth.

Though in his *Extensive Explanation of the "Shrīparamādya Tantra"*[29] Ānandagarbha treats the four sections of the *Compendium of Principles Tantra* that way at times, at other times he also relates the four sections to four types of objects of attainment required by every practitioner—the four Buddha Bodies (Nature, Fruition, Complete Enjoyment, and Emanation), the four exalted wisdoms (mirror-like, equality, individual realization, and achieving activities), and also the mind of enlightenment and the three perfections (of giving, wisdom, and effort). Also, with respect to the ordinary state Ānandagarbha correlates the four sections respectively with the basis-of-all,[a] afflicted intellect,[b] mental consciousness,[c] and sense consciousnesses[d] as well as with the four constituents—earth, water, fire, and wind—these being bases of purification. In these ways, the four sections are related to:

- the four Buddha Bodies and the four exalted wisdoms in terms of the fruits to be obtained
- the mind of enlightenment and three perfections in terms of the path
- the four consciousnesses and the four constituents in terms of the basic ordinary state.

In this sense, the four sections present the practice of one person. Thus, the four sections of the *Compendium of Principles Tantra* are treated sometimes in terms of four separate types of persons and at other times in terms of one individual.

About the four Buddha Bodies, Bu-dön describes the Nature Body as "The naturally pure sphere of reality undifferentiable from uncontaminated exalted wisdom, which has the same import as the Truth Body described elsewhere." He identifies the Nature Body—not as just the uncompounded state of separation from defilements or the natural purity from defilements, these being emptiness, the final mode of being of phenomena—but as like the innate exalted body discussed in Highest Yoga Tantra, this being the fundamental innate mind of clear light on the occasion of the fruitional

---

a *kun gzhi, ālaya.*

b *nyon yid, kliṣṭamanas.*

c *yid shes, manovijñāna.*

d *dbang shes, indriyavijñāna.*

level of Buddhahood, which is called the Truth Body. Concerning "uncontaminated exalted wisdom," the term "uncontaminated" has many meanings according to context; here, as in Chandrakīrti's *Supplement to (Nāgārjuna's) "Treatise on the Middle,"* uncontaminated exalted wisdom is one that directly realizes emptiness and is not polluted by ignorance or its predispositions—the finality of which is at Buddhahood. "Undifferentiable" means that object (the naturally pure sphere of reality, or emptiness) and subject (such exalted wisdom) are of one taste. This oneness of taste does not just refer to the fact that a consciousness is the same entity as its emptiness of inherent existence, for ignorance itself has a nature of emptiness of inherent existence. Rather, oneness of taste refers to an exalted wisdom that takes emptiness as its object of direct realization in an undifferentiable manner. Hence, the Nature Body is the final awareness realizing the noumenal nature, emptiness, in the manner of an undifferentiable entity.

Bu-dön identifies the Fruition Body as "an exalted body that is the final fruit of the two collections of merit and wisdom, adorned with the marks and beauties, authorized as the monarch of doctrine of the three realms." He identifies the Complete Enjoyment Body as "enjoying the complete holy doctrine, teaching the 84,000 bundles of doctrine," which is like, in Highest Yoga Tantra, calling fully endowed exalted speech "Complete Enjoyment Body"; this fits together with the third section of the *Compendium of Principles Tantra,* which is associated with the lineage of Amitābha and thus exalted speech. He identifies Emanation Bodies as "displaying various bodies in whatever way is appropriate to tame trainees." These are Emanation Bodies of beneficial activities; this fits together with the fourth section of the *Compendium of Principles Tantra,* which is associated with the lineage of Amoghasiddhi and thus exalted activities.

In brief, each of the four sections teaches practices, or paths, related to purifying respectively ordinary body, mind, speech, and activities into the exalted body, mind, speech, and activities on the effect stage of Buddhahood. The bases of purification are ordinary body, mind, speech, and activities as well as the basis-of-all, afflicted intellect, mental consciousness, and sense consciousnesses, and also the four constituents—earth, water, fire, and wind. The means of purification are respectively the four seals—great, pledge, doctrine, and action seals.[a] The effects of purification are respectively a Buddha's exalted body, mind, speech, and activities as well as the

[a] *phyag rgya chen po, mahāmudrā; dam tshig gi phyag rgya, samayamudrā; chos kyi phyag rgya, dharmamudrā; las kyi phyag rgya, karmamudrā.*

mirror-like wisdom, wisdom of equality, wisdom of individual realization, and wisdom of achieving activities (see chart next page).

The four maṇḍalas—great,[a] retention,[b] doctrine,[c] and action maṇḍalas[d]—respectively stress the four seals as means of purifying ordinary body, mind, speech, and activities into those of a Buddha. In the first section of the *Compendium of Principles Tantra:*

- The great maṇḍala emphasizes the great seal—or exalted body. In this maṇḍala the deities appear in physical form.
- The retention maṇḍala emphasizes the pledge seal—or exalted mind. In this maṇḍala though the central deity is the same (this being Vairochana in the first section), the deities are meditated in the form of hand-symbols—vajras, hooks, and so forth—which symbolize non-conceptual wisdom.
- The doctrine maṇḍala emphasizes the doctrine seal—or exalted speech. In this maṇḍala the hand-symbols of all but the central deity are meditated as being on their respective seats, with the deities themselves set in the middle of the hand-symbol in meditative equipoise. The deities have the aspect of single-pointed meditative stabilization of non-conceptual wisdom in meditative equipoise because it is in dependence on such meditative equipoise that the wheel of doctrine is turned.
- The action maṇḍala emphasizes the action seal—or exalted activities. In this maṇḍala, except for the five Ones-Gone-Thus, the deities are meditated in the aspect of goddesses of offering and so forth.

This is how the four maṇḍalas differ in presentation in the first section of the *Compendium of Principles Tantra.* For more detail you should study the root tantra, the explanatory tantras,[e] the commentaries by the Indian masters, and the explanation by Bu-d̄ön.

---

a *dkyil 'khor chen po, mahāmaṇḍala.*

b *gzungs kyi dkyil 'khor, dhāraṇīmaṇḍala.*

c *chos kyi dkyil 'khor, dharmamaṇḍala.*

d *las kyi dkyil 'khor, karmamaṇḍala.*

e The reference here includes the *Vajrashekhara Tantra,* which is the only explanatory tantra that covers the entire *Compendium of Principles* and is thus considered to be the main Yoga Tantra explanatory tantra. Lo-sang-chö-ḡyi-gyel-tsen speaks of the *Vajrashekhara Tantra* as a method explanatory tantra and speaks of the *Shrīparamādya Tantra* as a wisdom method explanatory tantra.

Sets of Fours

Section	*Lineage*	*Maṇḍala*	*Basis of purification*	*Affliction purified*	*Seal*	*Effect of purification*
Vajra Element	One-Gone-Thus (Vairochana)	great	body, basis-of-all, earth	desire	great seal	exalted body, mirror-like wisdom
Conquest over Three Realms	vajra (Akṣhobhya)	retention	mind, afflicted intellect, water	hatred	pledge seal	exalted mind, wisdom of equality
Taming Transmigrators	lotus (Amitābha)	doctrine	speech, mental consciousness, fire	obscuration/ wrong view	doctrine seal	exalted speech, wisdom of individual realization
Achieving Aims	jewel (Ratnasambhava) & action (Amoghasiddhi)	action	activity, sense consciousnesses, wind	miserliness	action seal	exalted activity, wisdom of achieving activities

When Ānandagarbha treats the great seal as exalted body, the pledge seal as exalted mind, the doctrine seal as exalted speech, and the action seal as exalted activity, it is within the context that all four sections are necessary for the practice of a *single* individual, since all practitioners must develop all four. Similarly, when Ānandagarbha and Buddhaguhya correlate the four sections with exalted body, mind, speech, and activities, it is within the context that all four sections are necessary for the practice of a *single* individual since all practitioners must develop these four. However, when they treat *each section* as also having the four seals and thus exalted body, mind, speech, and activity, it is within the framework of the four sections being for different individuals. In this latter way, each section emphasizes one from among exalted body, mind, speech, and activities, but it is not that the others are absent.

This is why impression of body, mind, speech, and activity with the four seals in order to enhance and exalt body, mind, speech, and activity is described in all four sections after the process of self-generation and the entry of the wisdom-being. Given that the three secrecies of a Buddha's body, speech, and mind are of one entity, even if there is an emphasis on one particular aspect, the others are not absent. For instance, with respect to *Guhyasamāja*[30] in Highest Yoga Tantra, when Akṣhobhya is the principal deity among the thirty-two deities of the maṇḍala, the maṇḍala itself is of the Akṣhobhya lineage, but this does not mean that Vairochana, Amitābha, Amoghasiddhi, and Ratnasambhava are not present in the maṇḍala; they are all there. The same is true when another deity serves as the principal deity in the maṇḍala.

2. Yoga With Signs

In all four tantras there are yogas with signs and yogas without signs. Yoga without signs occurs on the occasion of mainly meditating on emptiness, and yoga with signs, though usually involved with meditating on emptiness, is yoga when not mainly meditating on emptiness.

Coarse Yoga With Signs

As Den-ma-lo-chö's[a] short text on mantra says, there are:

1. those who, though permitted to meditate on Secret Mantra due to having received initiation, do not have the ability to do so. For instance, there are persons of dull faculties who, though they have received the full initiation of a vajra master, cannot perform the meditations.
2. those who have the ability to meditate on Secret Mantra but are not permitted because of not having been initiated. For instance, there are persons of sharp faculty who, though they are able to perform the meditations, have not received initiation.
3. those who both are permitted to meditate on Secret Mantra and have the ability
4. those who neither are permitted nor have the ability.

For those who have received initiation and are capable of meditation, there are two types of meditation—one for those who have received just a student's initiation and another for those with the full initiation of a master. The former involves self-generation as just one deity and thus is called "single yoga."[b] The latter involves self-generation along with many deities and is called "the great yoga of self-completion."[c]

A Student's Single Yoga

One who has received just the initiation of a student performs self-protection and then bathes. The *Vajrashekhara Tantra* describes four types

---

a *ldan ma blo chos,* late nineteenth and early twentieth centuries. The reference is likely to his short commentary on his teacher's *Grounds and Paths of Mantra.*

b *rnal 'byor gcig ldan.*

c *bdag rdzogs chen po'i rnal 'byor.*

of bathing—external, internal, secret, and suchness.[a] Then, having performed self-protection again as well as place-protection, you invite the deity, who is the basis for accumulating merit, in front of yourself. You pay obeisance from each of the four directions, disclose ill-deeds, admire the merit of all beings, entreat the deity to turn the wheel of doctrine, supplicate the deity not to pass into nirvāṇa, make worship of the twenty types, dedicate the virtue of these practices to the welfare of all beings, generate an altruistic intention to become enlightened, take refuge, assume the Bodhisattva vows, and so forth.

Then, you meditate on emptiness, this being the equivalent of bringing death to the path as the Truth Body in Highest Yoga Tantra. Here you be-

---

[a] Bu-d̄ön (*rdo 'byung 'grel chen;* aka *rdo rje dbyings kyi dkyil 'khor gyi cho ga rdo rje thams cad 'byung ba zhes bya ba'i rgya cher bshad pa,* Collected Works, vol. 11, 226.5-227.2) describes the four types of bathing: (Thanks to Steven Weinberger for the note.)

> Furthermore, there are four types of bathing: internal bathing, secret bathing, yogic bathing, and external bathing. The *Vajrashekhara Tantra* says:
>
> > Thoroughly perform the four bathings
> > Every day as much as you can.
> > I will explain in order
> > How a yogi performs bathing.
> >
> > Thoroughly abiding in the three vows
> > Is called the first bathing.
> > The second [bathing] is the disclosure [of misdeeds], supplication, and so forth
> > Set forth in the [*Compendium of Principles*] *Tantra.*
> >
> > Constructing mudrās is the third,
> > And the fourth and last is [bathing with] water.
>
> and the *Vajrashekhara Tantra* explains how the activity of bathing is done:
>
> > Taking the ten virtues as one's basis
> > Within having abandoned the ten non-virtues
> > And wanting to help elementals (*'byung ba, bhūta*)
> > Is asserted to be bathing having an internal nature.
> >
> > Seal-impressing yourself with seals
> > In order to thoroughly purify yourself
> > And correctly constructing all mudrās
> > Is called yogic bathing.
> >
> > Secret [bathing] is to promise to be endowed with the deeds,
> > Water bathing is a [physical] activity.
> > This activity is a washing/bathing of conceptuality.
> > These are to be done by vajra-masters.

come mindful of suchness, the absence of inherent existence; then, you meditate on two moon discs—the lower one marked with the sixteen vowels of the Sanskrit alphabet and the upper one marked with the thirty-six consonants, these being the thirty-three with the addition of *aḥ, laṃ,* and *kṣha.* Then, you imagine the full physical form of Vajrasattva. Because only a single deity is generated, the yoga is called "single yoga."

You cause the wisdom-being—the actual deity similar to whom you have imagined yourself—to enter the pledge-being, that is, yourself visualized as the deity. After this, you perform seal-impression with the four seals,[a] bestow initiation on yourself, make offering, pay homage to all Buddhas, and meditate on the great seal, that is to say, the divine body [which is your own body visualized as the exalted body of a deity]. You repeat mantra, maintaining this practice daily in four sessions for a year.

The self-generation mentioned just above is done by way of five rites, called the five manifest enlightenments.[b] These are the principles of mind, sattva, meditative stabilization, vajra, and Vajradhara:[c]

- First, you meditate on emptiness and then, within emptiness, meditate on a moon disc marked with the sixteen vowels. This is called the rite of the mind principle.[d]
- Then, you meditate on a second moon, above the former, marked with the thirty-six consonants—the rite of the sattva principle.[e]
- Then, you meditate on a vajra [on top of the second moon], this being the rite of the meditative stabilization principle.[f]
- This turns into the appropriate hand-symbol—the rite of the vajra principle.[g]
- These transform into the full body of the deity—the rite of the great seal, or Vajradhara, principle.[h] The wisdom-being is caused to enter the

---

a For a description of how to do the four seals, see the next section and also 128ff.

b The practice that follows is drawn from the enlightenment narrative at the beginning of the *Compendium of Principles Tantra,* which in commentarial literature is called the five manifest enlightenments (*mngon byang lnga*). (Thanks to Steven Weinberger for the note.)

c For detailed descriptions of the five manifest enlightenments see 123ff. and 154ff.

d *sems kyi de kho na nyid.*

e *sems dpa'i de kho na nyid.*

f *ting nge 'dzin gyi de kho na nyid.*

g *rdo rje'i de kho na nyid.*

h *rdo rje 'chang gi de kho na nyid.*

> imagined deity, and seal impression with the four seals—pledge, doctrine, action, and great seals—is done.[a]

Due to there being just the single central deity, this is called the single yoga and not the great yoga of self-completion.

That is the way self-generation is described in Ānandagarbha's commentary on the first part[b] of the *Compendium of Principles Tantra.* In the same author's *Means of Achievement Called "Source of Vajrasattva"*[c] in two versions—shorter and longer—a practitioner, as before, does the single yoga, but then sets himself or herself as the deity in space and as a basis for that deity imagines spheres of the four elements—earth, water, fire, and wind—with Mount Meru and an inestimable mansion on top. In the mansion is a lion seat, onto which the practitioner, as the deity in space, descends; you thereby mimic the descent of a deity.

---

[a] Seal-impression is described in the next section.

[b] In Tibetan canons Ānandagarbha's commentary on the *Compendium of Principles Tantra,* the *Illumination of the Principles* (*de kho na nyid snang ba, tattvālokakāri;* P3333, vols. 71-72; Toh. 2510, vol. *li*) is in two parts, called commentary on the first part (*stod 'grel*) and commentary on the second part (*smad 'grel*), as is his commentary on the *Shrīparamādya.* Bu-d̄ön (*rnal 'byor rgyud gyi rgya mtshor 'jug pa'i gru gzings,* in Collected Works, vol. 11, 148.7ff.) reports that Rin-chen-sang-b̄o (*rin chen bzang po*) had trouble finding these two texts in Kashmir. He obtained the first part and second part at different times, and so translated them at different times. The *Shrīparamādya Tantra* itself was also translated in two parts at two different times by two different translator teams, and in fact this tantra appears in the various editions of the Kangyur as *two* separate texts (P119/ Toh. 487 and P120/ Toh. 488) which, according to their respective colophons, were translated by different translators. This is the likely reason for the epithets "commentary on the first [part]" and "commentary on the second [part]." (Thanks to Steven Weinberger for the note.)

[c] The longer version is *rdo rje sems dpa' 'byung ba zhes bya ba'i sgrub thabs, vajrasattvodayanāmasādhana,* P3340, vol. 74 and Toh. 2517; the shorter version is *rdo rje sems dpa'i sgrub pa'i thabs, vajrasattvasādhana,* P3341, vol. 74 and Toh. 2518. About the two means of achievement of Vajrasattva composed by Ānandagarbha, Bu-d̄ön (*rnal 'byor rgyud kyi rgya mtshor 'jug pa'i gru gzings,* in *Collected Works,* vol. 11, 124.4-124.5) says:

> [Ānandagarbha] composed the *Means of Achievement Called "The Source of Vajrasattva,"* the length of the text being two hundred and fifty stanzas. He composed the *Means of Achievement of Vajrasattva,* the tripartite rite [the three meditative stabilizations] which relies on the single yoga of Vajrasattva. These two means of achievement are the extensive way and the condensed way, known [respectively] as the longer *Source of [Vajra]sattva* and the shorter *Source of [Vajra]sattva* (*sems dpa' 'byung chen/'byung chung du grags so/*).

(Thanks to Steven Weinberger for the note.)

Then, according to the longer *Means of Achievement Called "Source of Vajrasattva"* you say, for instance, "*vajradhātu,*" construct the hand-seal of supreme enlightenment, generate yourself as the appropriate deity—Vairochana, for instance—and then saying "*vajrasattva,*" emanate from the heart a Vajrasattva, setting him on a lion throne, which is similar to your own, in front of yourself. This is like deity generation in front. Reciting the essence-mantra of Vajrasattva and constructing his hand-seal, you contemplate yourself as Vajrasattva. With mantra and hand-seal, you mentally open the four doors of the maṇḍala and summon the Buddhas, whom you praise with the hundred and eight names, considering them all to be Vajrasattva. Having summoned the wisdom-being and caused the wisdom-being to enter yourself you make seal-impression with the four seals—the great seal and so forth—and make offering. Then, you meditate on the three equalities—that is, meditate on emptiness in signless yoga, viewing (1) yourself, (2) all sentient beings, and (3) all the deities of the maṇḍala as equally without self—that is, without inherent existence. You view all phenomena as of one taste in the sphere of the absence of inherent existence. Then, you repeat mantra. This type of single yoga, in which only one basic deity is generated, is described for students and is the format of both the longer and shorter *Means of Achievement Called "Source of Vajrasattva"* by Ānandagarbha.

Seal-Impression

As Ḏzong-ka-ḇa's student Ke-drup (see 131) says:

> Seal-impression with the four seals is done after you have generated yourself as the pledge-being and caused the wisdom-being to enter into the pledge-being.

Each section of the *Compendium of Principles Tantra* describes the four maṇḍalas—great, retention, doctrine, and action maṇḍalas—which emphasize the respective four seals—great, pledge, doctrine, and action seals. The four seals are respectively correlated to purifying ordinary body, mind, speech, and activities into exalted body, mind, speech, and activities (see chart, 32).

About seal-impression of body, mind, speech, and activities, which is required for both the student's and the master's yoga, the *Annotations for the "Purification of [All] Bad Transmigrations Tantra" from the Speech of the*

Foremost [D̄zong-ka-b̄a],[a] written by Gyel-d̄eng-b̄a Dön-drup-b̄el, is very helpful. It says:

> The bases of purification are body, speech, mind, and activities of the basic [or ordinary] state. Through purifying these with the four seals of the path, the four seals [or] bodies of the fruit are accomplished. Therefore, all the essentials of the path must be extractable from within [the topic of] seal-impression with the four seals. Due to this, the three—body, speech, and mind—as well as the activities of the practitioner are the bases of seal-impression.

The present ordinary body, speech, mind, and activities of the practitioner are both the bases of purification and bases to be impressed with the four seals. He continues:

> If the seals that are the means of impression were held to be only seals [that is, gestures made] by the hands, it would be of little import. Hence, there are two [types of seals, internal and external], the first of which are internal seals. The practitioner's body generated [that is, imagined] as this or that deity is the great seal.

The internal great seal is taken to be body—the generation and clear imagination of yourself as having the exalted body of a deity of the Vajra Element Maṇḍala, for instance.

> Meditation on an original[b] five-pointed vajra on a moon [disc] at the heart is the [internal] pledge seal [of exalted mind]. The [internal] doctrine seal [of exalted speech] is [meditation on] a vajra on the tongue in the throat with the letter of doctrine set in its middle. Contemplation of a variegated [that is, crossed] vajra at the heart is the internal action seal [of exalted activities].
>
> The four external seals are constructions of four hand-seals

---

a *ngan song sbyong ba'i rgyud rje'i gsung gi mchan dang bcas pa* written down by *rgyal stengs pa don grub dpal;* in *The Collected Works of rJe Tsoṅ-kha-pa blo-bzaṅ-grags-pa,* vol. 15 (New Delhi: Ngawang Gelek Demo, 1975), 269-453; the passage cited is 351-353 (vol. *tha,* 42a.4-43a.1). The Sanskrit and Tibetan texts of the two redactions of the *Purification of All Bad Transmigrations Tantra,* along with an English translation of one of them, can be found in Tadeusz Skorupski, *The Sarvadurgatipariśodhana Tantra: Elimination of All Evil Destinies* (New Delhi: Motilal Banarsidass, 1983).

b For the meaning of "original" see below, 125.

[that is, physical gestures] at the time of seal-impression with the four internal seals.[a]

With respect to the meaning of "impression," when[31] the external and the internal great seals are constructed, you imagine that all the minute particles of your own body have become undifferentiable from all parts of the exalted body of a One-Gone-Thus. When the external and internal pledge seals are constructed, you imagine your own mind to be undifferentiable from the exalted mind of a Buddha. When the external and internal doctrine seals are constructed, you imagine your speech and the exalted speech of a Buddha to be undifferentiable. When the external and internal action seals are constructed, you imagine your activities of the three doors [of body, speech, and mind] and the exalted activities of exalted body, speech, and mind of a Buddha to be undifferentiable.

Thus, impression means that upon constructing the four external and internal seals, you view your own body, mind, speech, and activities to be those of the Buddha who is your object of attainment.

With respect to the etymology of "seal": seal,[b] sign,[c] symbol,[d] and mark[e] are equivalent, and hence, a seal is so called because it symbolizes or causes mindfulness. [Seals make you] mindful that the effect seals—the Truth Body and Form Body with their branches, exalted activities—are undifferentiable from the bases of impression.

Or, in another way, seals are so called because through the bases of impression being impressed with those means of impression it is difficult for you to pass beyond being undifferentiable from the deity, just as, for example, subjects cannot deviate from the seal marking a king's law. It is as the "Continuation of the

---

[a] As examples of the four seals, see those of Vajrasattva (seals 1-4). The doctrine seal of Vajrasattva that is depicted there is for those mainly performing yoga without signs, which is the hand-configuration of meditative equipoise. The doctrine seal of Vajrasattva for those mainly performing yoga with signs is the same as the great seal of Vajrasattva.

[b] *phyag rgya, mudrā.*

[c] *rtags, liṅga.*

[d] *mtshan nyid, lakṣaṇa.*

[e] *mtshan ma, nimitta.*

Compendium of Principles Tantra" says,[32] "Just as the word of law [impressed] with the supreme royal seal cannot be broken...."

Objection: If such is the meaning of seal-impression, its purpose is achieved by the internal seals, in which case the construction of hand-seals would not be necessary.

Answer: It is not so, for Buddhaguhya's *Introduction to the Meaning of the [Compendium of Principles] Tantra*[33] explains the meaning of [a passage from] the *Shrīparamādya* as follows:

> For example, solitary mind separate from body is like space—devoid of activities of going, coming, and so forth. Solitary body separate from mind is like a wall, due to which its activities cannot be achieved. When the two, body and mind, assemble and assist each other, their respective activities are accomplished. Similarly, when the two—external and internal seals—accompany each other as assisters, their mutual activities are achieved. The *Shrīparamādya* says:
>
> > Mind is empty like an illusion;
> > Separate from body, it cannot achieve.
> > Body also is like a wall;
> > Separate from mind it is without activity.
> > Similarly the yoga of seals....

Mind separate from body cannot openly display activities; body separate from mind is the same. Rather, actions must be done upon the aggregation of mind and body. Just so, here when practicing techniques for transforming basic—or ordinary—body, speech, mind, and activities into those of the fruit stage of Buddhahood, it is necessary both to cultivate (1) internal meditative stabilization on a divine body, on a vajra on a moon disc at the heart, on a seed syllable on a vajra in the throat, and on a vajra at the heart, and (2) at the same time to construct the appropriate gesture, or seal, with the hands. These must be done in unison, for it is said in Yoga Tantra ritual texts that if you fail to construct seals with the hands, the rite is nullified. Unlike on other occasions, it is not just that if the hand-seals are constructed, it is better, but if not, there is no fault of nullifying the rite. Here, they must be done.[a]

---

[a] For more explanation of the four seals see 128ff.

A Master's Great Yoga of Self-Completion

A master performs not only the single yoga but also the great yoga of self-completion, meditating on the full complement of deities in the respective maṇḍala. The great yoga of self-completion is a complete self-generation, beginning with bathing and so forth. You imagine the whole maṇḍala in your own body—the basic body being generated as Vajrasattva, for instance—and then [in meditation] receive full initiation, make offerings, and so forth. The pattern of the meditation does not follow that of thoroughly afflicted phenomena—the bases of purification—in the sense of mimicking the pattern of death, intermediate state, and rebirth within meditation, for such occurs only in Highest Yoga Tantra. However, the meditation is in the pattern of the production of very pure phenomena in the sense that it mimics the pattern of the meditation of Bodhisattvas in their last lifetime. It follows the procedure of the alternating and leap-over meditations performed, for instance, by Shākyamuni [prior to his full enlightenment]. The cultivation of the paths for becoming a Buddha by way of the five manifest enlightenments accords with Shākyamuni's gaining full enlightenment by way of these five, generating the four concentrations and four formless absorptions—limitless space, limitless consciousness, nothingness, and peak of cyclic existence—in forward order and then generating them in reverse order, after which you again ascend, but skipping, for instance, the second concentration, leaping over levels of meditative stabilization. At the end of these, you imitate the final step in becoming enlightened, the vajra-like meditative stabilization at the end of the continuum of being a sentient being [who has obstructions yet to be abandoned].[a]

---

[a] Bu-dön describes the process in detail in his *Ship for Launching onto the Ocean of Yoga Tantra* (Collected Works, vol. 11, 8.5–9.7) (text from *Compendium of Principles Tantra* itself is in boldface type):

> Then [i.e., having generated the mind for enlightenment and received the Bodhisattva trainings], **he became a Bodhisattva—*bodhi*** means "**wisdom**"; ***sattva*** means "**method**"—**endowed with method and wisdom, at which point** he donned the armor for the sake of sentient beings **with the great enthusiasm** of mental effort. Having taken various births over three periods of countless eons, for the sake of others he accumulated the collections of merit and wisdom through **performing innumerable very fantastic**, wonderful **difficult deeds**—giving away his kingdom, his life, and so forth—through which he, beginning from the grounds of engagement through belief, progressed **step by step** over the ten [Bodhisattva] grounds.

In the rite for a master, but not for a student, the practitioner draws in the beings of bad transmigrations and removes the ill-deeds in their mental continuums. It is at the point of this practice in the *Compendium of Principles Tantra* that the *Sarvavid Vairochana Tantra*—that is, the *Purification of All Bad Transmigrations Tantra*—is set forth. This practice of drawing in beings from bad transmigrations and removing their ill-deeds does not appear in the two *Means of Achievement* by Ānandagarbha since they were written for those on the student level.

Through that [i.e., progressing over the Bodhisattva grounds], **he attained well [everything] up to bestowal of initiation** of the tenth [ground], whereupon he entered the preparation for the first concentration called the not unable, the first concentration, the special actual first concentration, the second concentration, the third concentration, the fourth concentration, the sphere of limitless space, the sphere of limitless consciousness, the sphere of nothingness, and the sphere of neither-discrimination-nor-non-discrimination.

Then he entered [the concentrations] in reverse order, from the peak of cyclic existence through to the not unable [the preparation for the first concentration]. Then, putting aside [i.e., skipping] every other one, he [proceeded in leap-over fashion]: from the not unable, he entered the special [actual first] concentration; from there, the third concentration; from there, limitless space; from there, nothingness; and from there, the meditative stabilization of the peak of cyclic existence. Then he also [proceeded] in reverse order: from the peak of cyclic existence, he entered limitless consciousness; from there, the fourth concentration; from there, the second concentration; from there, the mere actual first concentration; and from there, the not unable. Then he also [proceeded this way]: from the not unable, he entered the mere actual first concentration; from there, the special actual first concentration; from there, the second concentration; and from there, the third concentration. From the third concentration, he entered the small of the small of the fourth concentration. Then he engaged in meditative absorption of and actualized the middling of the small [of the fourth concentration], the great of the small [of the fourth concentration], the small of the middling [of the fourth concentration], the middling of the middling [of the fourth concentration], the great of the middling [of the fourth concentration], the small of the great [of the fourth concentration], the middling of the great [of the fourth concentration], and the great of the great [of the fourth concentration], whereby in dependence upon just accepting to do all activities for the sake of thoroughly completing the collections, he achieved them, whereupon he became a Bodhisattva in his last lifetime [before becoming a Buddha] called "Bodhisattva Sarvārthasiddhi."

(Thanks to Steven Weinberger for the note.)

Three Meditative Stabilizations

With respect to the yoga to be used to actualize the state of a Vairochana, each of the four sections of the *Compendium of Principles Tantra* sets forth three types of meditative stabilizations, called initial preparation,[a] supreme royal maṇḍala,[b] and supreme royal activities.[c] Those taught in the first section, the "Vajra Element," have Vairochana as the main deity; those in the second, "Conquest over the Three Realms," Huṃkara; those in the third, "Taming Transmigrators," Amitābha; those in the fourth, "Achieving Aims," Amoghasiddhi. Each of these, in turn, is presented in extensive, middling, and brief forms in relation to practitioners who want practices of those lengths. Again, the extensive meditative stabilizations of all three types—initial preparation, supreme royal maṇḍala, and supreme royal activities—are taught in four different places in each of the central maṇḍalas in each of the four sections (see chart next page).

In order to bestow initiation on another, a master must perform either an extensive, middling, or brief approximation. The extensive approximation entails cultivating the three meditative stabilizations—initial preparation, supreme royal maṇḍala, and supreme royal activities[d]—without omitting anything. The middling, according to Bu-d̄ön's *Extensive Explanation of (Ānandagarbha's) "Source of All Vajras": Wish-Granting Jewel,*[34] is an abbreviated form of the emanation of deities in the supreme royal maṇḍala.

In the more extensive format:

- the central Vairochana emanates the sixteen male Bodhisattvas
- then the Ones-Gone-Thus in the four directions emanate the four female Bodhisattvas, called Perfection Goddesses, beginning with Sattvavajrī
- then Vairochana emanates the four inner or secret offering goddesses, beginning with Vajralāsye

---

a *dang po sbyor ba'i ting nge 'dzin, ādiyogasamādhi.*

b *dkyil 'khor rgyal mchog gi ting nge 'dzin, maṇḍalarājāgrīsamādhi.*

c *las rgyal mchog gi ting nge 'dzin, karmarājāgrīsamādhi.*

d Initial preparation includes all the activities starting with using the exalted wisdom of emptiness as the ground out of which the maṇḍala is emanated, through to and including generation of oneself as the central deity. Supreme royal maṇḍala consists of emanating the full complement of maṇḍala deities. Supreme royal activities encompasses all rites and compassionate activities subsequent to emanation of the maṇḍala.

Seventy-two Meditative Stabilizations

(18 are described in each of the four sections of the *Compendium of Principles*)

Vajra Element Section[a]
- initial preparation meditative stabilization
  - extensive
    - in part on great maṇḍala (1)
    - in part on retention maṇḍala (2)
    - in part on doctrine maṇḍala (3)
    - in part on action maṇḍala (4)
  - middling—in part on four-seal maṇḍala (5)
  - brief—in part on single-seal maṇḍala (6)
- supreme royal meditative stabilization
  - extensive
    - in part on great maṇḍala (7)
    - in part on retention maṇḍala (8)
    - in part on doctrine maṇḍala (9)
    - in part on action maṇḍala (10)
  - middling—in part on four-seal maṇḍala (11)
  - brief—in part on single-seal maṇḍala (12)
- supreme royal activities meditative stabilization
  - extensive
    - in part on great maṇḍala (13)
    - in part on retention maṇḍala (14)
    - in part on doctrine maṇḍala (15)
    - in part on action maṇḍala (16)
  - middling—in part on four-seal maṇḍala (17)
  - brief—in part on single-seal maṇḍala (18)

[a] The same list of eighteen is to be applied to the other three sections—Conquest over Three Realms, Taming Transmigrators, and Achieving Aims.

- then the Ones-Gone-Thus of the four directions emanate the four outer offering goddesses, Vajradhūpe and so forth, in series
- then the central Vairochana also emanates the four door-keepers.

In this way, in the extensive form the deities of the maṇḍala are emanated gradually in order, whereas in the middling form the Ones-Gone-Thus of the four directions emanate the deities of their particular quarter all at once. The latter accords with the mode of procedure set forth in the *Compendium of Principles Tantra* at the point of the maṇḍala of the four seals in connection with the reciting of five mantras. The brief approximation, on the other hand, requires just the great yoga of self-completion with a thousand repetitions of the mantra of each deity of the maṇḍala.

Even just to achieve a deity, a master must cultivate not only the great yoga of self-completion but also the three meditative stabilizations—initial preparation, supreme royal maṇḍala, and supreme royal activities in, at least, the brief format. These three meditative stabilizations are qualitatively similar to the effect state of Buddhahood and are the chief paths for becoming fully enlightened into the Three Bodies of a Buddha. Thus, a master must, at the least, cultivate the three meditative stabilizations in abbreviated form as well as the great yoga, which does not have extensive, middling and brief forms.

When performing approximation either as a student or as a master, you must meditate until clear appearance of the deity and the pride of being that deity become firm. This is the measure of initially generating the yoga in your continuum.

This system of practice is described for those capable of engaging in single-pointed meditation over months and years until clear appearance is developed. Those who cannot do such recite the ritual formulation, pretending that all of the prescribed steps are occurring in fact. Although this is designated with the name "meditation," the procedure is very different, the emphasis here being on repetition of mantra. Those who perform tantric rites must at least have this level of practice.

Persons who cannot succeed at any of these practices include:

- those who have not generated the altruistic intention to become enlightened
- those who have doubts with respect to Mantra
- those who do not practice in accordance with the lama's explanation, or

- those who, even though they may not have doubts about Mantra, do not have strong faith wishing to practice.

Such persons cannot achieve mantric feats. As mentioned earlier (23), you should develop a fully qualified altruistic intention to become enlightened, or at least a deeply felt altruistic intention. Dzong-ka-ba mentions that you must eradicate doubt and two-mindedness, which, though they usually mean the same thing, may here indicate, respectively, doubt tending to the fact and doubt not tending to the fact, or levels of strength of doubt. Or, if we take them as synonymous, the repetition of two words having the same meaning emphasizes the need for single-pointedness of mind—the need to be unwavering. In any case, you must be without doubt regarding the tantras and have faith in the deity and the lama. Still, even if a person has completely overcome doubt and has attained the faith of conviction in these topics but does not have a strong wish to generate those qualities, that person cannot succeed in the practice of Mantra.

MEDITATION ON A SUBTLE OBJECT

Meditative stabilization on a subtle object—meditation on a tiny hand-symbol—has some of the same purposes as in the Highest Yoga Tantra practice of meditating on a tiny hand-symbol at the lower and upper openings of the central channel. Thus, from this viewpoint also the *Compendium of Principles Tantra* has connection with the *Guhyasamāja Tantra.*

Here the subtle object is a five-pointed vajra, which at the smallest is the size of the tip of a single hair and at the largest is the size of a grain of sesame. Its color is the same as that of the deity being meditated. It is first generated at the navel area or the heart, then is drawn up to the nose and is contemplated standing at the tip of the nose.

Contemplating a tiny vajra at the tip of the nose as the object of observation, a yogi achieves single-pointed meditative stabilization, which is not interrupted by even subtle laxity or subtle excitement, such that the object is seen clearly as if in direct perception. It is achieved through skill in using mindfulness and introspection as explained in Kamalashīla's three works on the *Stages of Meditation*[35] and in Dzong-ka-ba's longer and shorter *Expositions of the Stages of the Path*[36] in the sections on achieving calm abiding.[a] Let us consider this process of developing a strongly concentrated mind.

---

[a] *zhi gnas, śamatha.*

Process of Achieving Calm Abiding

Calm abiding is predominantly stabilizing meditation, in which the mind is kept on a single object, rather than analytical meditation, in which a topic such as impermanence or emptiness is analyzed with reasoning. The purpose of developing calm abiding is that since a mind that is scattered to external objects is relatively powerless, the mind needs to be concentrated in order to become powerful. If you do not have concentration in which the mind is unfluctuatingly stable and clear, the faculty of wisdom cannot know its object, just as it is, in all its subtleties. Therefore, it is necessary to have a highly focused mind. Furthermore, even though you have mere concentration, it cannot harm the misconception that objects exist in and of themselves. A union of concentration and the wisdom realizing the emptiness of inherent existence is needed.

In the Mantra Vehicle in general and in Yoga Tantra in particular, many techniques for facilitating achievement of calm abiding are described; first let us consider techniques shared with all systems. Physical posture is important. Sit with your legs crossed. Set the backbone as straight as an arrow. Place your shoulders level and your hands in the position of meditative equipoise, four finger-widths below the navel, with the left hand on the bottom, right hand on top, and your thumbs touching to form a triangle. Bending the neck down slightly, like a peacock's, allow the mouth and teeth to be as usual, with the tip of the tongue touching the roof of the mouth near the front teeth. Let the eyes gaze downwards loosely—it is not necessary that they be directed to the end of the nose; they can be pointed toward the floor in front of you if this seems more natural. Do not open the eyes too wide nor forcefully close them; leave them open a little. Even with them open, when your mental consciousness becomes steady upon its object, appearances to your eye consciousness will not disturb you but will go unnoticed. Still, it is suitable if sometimes they close of their own accord.

In order to set the mind steadily on an object of observation, it is necessary initially to use an object of observation suited to counteracting your own predominant afflictive emotion, since its force remains with your mind now and can easily interrupt any attempt to concentrate the mind. Therefore, Buddha described many types of objects for purifying behavior:

- For someone whose predominant afflictive emotion is desire, ugliness is a helpful object of meditation. Here, "ugliness" does not necessarily refer to distorted forms; the very nature of our body—composed of blood, flesh, bone, and so forth—might seem superficially to be very beautiful with a good color, solid and yet soft to touch, but when it is investigated, you see that its essence is quite different—substances like bone, blood, urine, feces, and so forth.

- For someone who has predominantly engaged in hatred, the object of meditation is love.
- For someone who was predominantly sunk in obscuration, the meditation is on the twelve links of the dependent-arising of cyclic existence because contemplating its complexity promotes intelligence.
- For someone whose predominant afflictive emotion is pride, the meditation could be on the divisions of the constituents because, when meditating on the many divisions, you get to the point where you realize that there are many things you do not know, thereby lessening an inflated sense of yourself.
- Those dominated by conceptuality can observe the exhalation and inhalation of the breath because by tying the mind to the breath discursiveness diminishes.

A particularly helpful object for all personality types is a Buddha body, since concentration on a Buddha's body causes your mind to mix with virtuous qualities. No matter what the object is, this is not a case of meditating within looking at an external object with your eyes but of causing an image of it to appear to the mental consciousness.

For instance, if you are to concentrate on a Buddha body, first you need to come to know it well through hearing it described or through looking at a picture or statue, getting used to it so that it can appear clearly to the mind. Then, imagine it about four feet in front of you, at the height of your eyebrows, about two inches high. It should be meditated as being clear, with a nature of brilliant light; this helps to prevent the onset of laxity, a condition in which the mind's mode of apprehension is too loose. Also, you can consider the imagined Buddha body to be heavy; this helps to prevent excitement, a condition in which the mind's mode of apprehension is too tight. In addition, as much as you can reduce the size of the object, so much does it help in withdrawing the mind, channeling it. Once the object originally has been determined, you may not change its nature or size; it must be fixed for the duration of generating calm abiding.

First cause the object to appear to your mind. Then, hold it with mindfulness such that you do not lose it. Mindfulness itself is a faculty of non-forgetfulness that causes the mind not to scatter to other objects; it is what keeps the mind on its object of observation without becoming distracted to something else. It needs to be trained and enhanced by repeatedly putting the mind back on the object.

Along with holding the visualized object of observation with mindfulness, you inspect, as if from a corner, to see whether the object is clear and stable; the faculty that engages in this inspection is called introspection. Although when powerful steady mindfulness is achieved, introspection is generated, the uncommon function of introspection is to further inspect from time to time to see whether the mind has come under the influence of excitement or laxity. This is because while keeping on the object, your mind must have two qualities:

- great clarity of both the object and the consciousness itself
- staying one-pointedly on the object of observation.

Two factors prevent these from developing—laxity and excitement. Laxity prevents the development of clarity, and excitement prevents the stability of staying with the object.

That which interferes with the steadiness of the object of observation and causes it to fluctuate is excitement, which includes any scattering of the mind to an object other than the object of meditation. To stop that, withdraw your mind more strongly inside so that the intensity of the mode of apprehension of the object begins to lower. If you need a further technique to withdraw the mind, it helps to leave the object of meditation temporarily and think about something that makes you more sober, such as the imminence of death. Such reflections can cause your heightened mode of apprehension of the object, the mind's being too tight, to lower or loosen somewhat, whereby you are better able to stay on the object of observation.

It is not sufficient just to have stability; clarity is also needed. That which prevents clarity is laxity, which is a case of the mind's becoming too relaxed, too loose, lacking intensity—the tautness of the mind having become weak, caused by over-withdrawal inside. Heaviness of mind and body can lead to becoming lax, which can lead to a type of lethargy in which, losing the object of observation, you have as if fallen into darkness; this can lead even to sleep. When this begins to occur, it is necessary to raise, to heighten, this excessive declination of the mind by making it more taut, more tight. If you need a further technique to accomplish this, it helps to brighten the object of meditation or, if that does not work, to leave the object of meditation temporarily and think on something that makes you joyous, such as the wonderful opportunity that a human lifetime affords for spiritual practice. If that does not work, you can even leave off meditating and go to a high place or where there is a vast view. Such techniques cause your deflated mind to heighten, to sharpen.

While holding the object of observation with mindfulness, investigate with introspection from time to time to see whether the mind has come under the influence of laxity or excitement. It is necessary within your own experience to recognize when the mode of apprehension has become too excited or too lax and determine the best practice for lowering or heightening it. In time, your will develop a sense of the proper level of tautness of the mind such that you will be able to catch laxity and excitement just before they arise and prevent their arising.

As you practice this way, the mind gradually develops more and more stability and clarity. The progression is described in terms of:

- levels of progress called the nine mental abidings[a] (setting the mind, continuous setting, resetting, close setting, disciplining, pacifying, thorough pacifying, making one-pointed, and setting in equipoise)
- mental faculties called the six powers[b] (hearing, thinking, mindfulness, introspection, effort, and familiarity)
- styles of fixing on the object called the four mental engagements[c] (forcible, interrupted, uninterrupted engagement, and effortless engagement)
- difficulties called the five faults[d] (laziness, forgetting the object, not identifying laxity and excitement, not applying antidotes to laxity and excitement, and over-applying antidotes to laxity and excitement)
- remedies for those defects called the eight antidotes[e] (faith, aspiration, effort, and pliancy, which are antidotes to laziness; mindfulness, which is the antidote to forgetting the object; introspection, which is the antidote to non-identification of laxity and excitement; application, which is the antidote to not applying antidotes to laxity and excitement; and desisting from over-applying antidotes).

The first mental abiding, setting the mind,[f] occurs when you initially

---

a *sems gnas dgu, navākārā cittasthiti.*

b *stobs, bala.*

c *yid la byed pa, manaskāra.*

d *nyes dmigs, ādīnava.*

e *'du byed pa, abhisaṃskāra.*

f *sems 'jog pa, cittasthāpana.*

withdraw the mind inside and place it on the object of observation, not letting it scatter to external objects. This is a result of the first power—hearing instructions on how to set the mind on an object of observation. At that time, the mind, for the most part, cannot stay in place, and thoughts come one after another like a waterfall. Due to this, you come to identify thoughts and even wonder whether conceptuality is increasing. However, the seeming cascade of thoughts is due to not having previously identified the extent of your own thoughts, since you had not directed the mind inward, whereas now you notice them due to employing mindfulness.

With gradual cultivation, you develop the continuum of placement on the object. Through the second power—thinking—you are able to maintain a slight continuum of placement on the object, at which point the second mental abiding, called "continuous setting,"[a] occurs. At that time, thought sometimes is pacified and sometimes suddenly arises; you have the sense that conceptuality is resting a little. During these first two states, the main problems from among the five faults are laziness[b] and forgetfulness,[c] but laxity[d] and excitement[e] are also plentiful, since a continuum of meditative stabilization occurs only infrequently. Since you have to strive to force the mind to aim at its object, this is a period of the first of the four mental engagements, forcible engagement.[f]

Gradually you immediately recognize distraction through the third power—mindfulness[g]—and place it back on the object. At this point, the third mental abiding, called resetting,[h] occurs. Then, the power of mindfulness matures, due to which you are not distracted from the object of observation. This is the fourth mental abiding, called "close setting."[i]

By the power of introspection[j]—the fourth power—you realize the faults of conceptuality and of scattering to afflictive emotions, due to which the mind does not suffer these. Taking joy in the good qualities of

---

a *rgyun du 'jog pa, saṃsthāpana.*

b *le lo, kausīdya.*

c *gdams ngag brjed pa, avavādasammoṣa.*

d *bying ba, laya.*

e *rgod pa, auddhatya.*

f *sgrim ste 'jug pa, balavāhana.*

g *dran pa, smṛti.*

h *slan te 'jog pa, avasthāpana.*

i *nye bar 'jog pa, upasthāpana.*

j *shes bzhin, saṃprajanya.*

meditative stabilization, you attain the fifth mental abiding called "disciplining."[a]

Next, through the power of introspection you know the disadvantages of distraction and so forth, and you stop any dislike of meditative stabilization, at which point the sixth mental abiding, called "pacifying,"[b] arises.

Then, through effort[c]—the fifth power—as soon as desire, scattering, laxity, lethargy, or the like is produced in even subtle form, you abandon it through exertion. At this point, the seventh mental abiding, called "thorough pacifying,"[d] occurs. During the third through seventh mental abidings, even if the stability of meditative stabilization predominates, it is interrupted by laxity and excitement, due to which these are states of interrupted engagement.[e]

Then, through the power of effort and by merely employing mindfulness and introspection at the beginning of the session, discordant factors such as laxity and excitement are unable to interrupt meditative stabilization, which, therefore, is produced continuously. At this point the eighth mental abiding, called "making one-pointed,"[f] arises. Since laxity and excitement are unable to interrupt meditation, you are able to sustain meditative stabilization for a long time, due to which this is an occasion of uninterrupted mental engagement.[g]

Then, through the sixth power, thorough familiarity,[h] the exertion of implementing mindfulness and introspection is no longer needed, and the mind engages the object of observation of its own accord, due to which this is an occasion of spontaneous engagement.[i] At this point, the ninth mental abiding, called "setting in equipoise,"[j] is gained. When at the start of a session you set your mind on the object of observation, meditative stabilization is sustained uninterruptedly for a long time through its own force, without needing to rely on exertion.

---

a *dul bar byed pa, damana.*

b *zhi bar byed pa, śamana.*

c *brtson 'grus, vīrya.*

d *nye bar zhi bar byed pa, vyupaśamana.*

e *bar du chad cing 'jug pa, sacchidravāhana.*

f *rtse gcig tu byed pa, ekotīkaraṇa.*

g *chad pa med par 'jug pa, nischidravāhana.*

h *yongs su 'dris pa, paricaya.*

i *lhun grub tu 'jug pa, anābhogavāhana.*

j *mnyam par 'jog pa, samādhāna.*

This ninth mental abiding in which the mind becomes entirely and effortlessly absorbed in meditative stabilization is a similitude of calm abiding, but not actual calm abiding. Eventually, through the power of stabilizing meditation in which the mind is set one-pointedly on its object of observation, an initial mental pliancy—a serviceability of mind—is generated. As a sign that mental pliancy is about to be generated, a tingly sensation is felt at the top of the head. This pleasant feeling is compared to that of a warm hand placed on top of the head after it has been shaved. When mental pliancy has been generated, a favorable wind, or energy, circulates in the body, engendering physical pliancy. Through this wind, or air, pervading the entire body, the unserviceability of the body such that it cannot be directed to virtuous activities in accordance with your wishes is removed. The generation of physical pliancy, in turn, engenders a bliss of physical pliancy, a sense of comfort throughout the body due to the power of meditative stabilization.

The bliss of physical pliancy induces a bliss of mental pliancy, making the mind blissful. At first, this joyous mental bliss is a little too buoyant, but then gradually it becomes more steady; at this point, one attains an unfluctuating pliancy. This marks attainment of a fully qualified meditative stabilization of calm abiding.

Developing Meditative Dexterity in Yoga Tantra

To induce meditative stabilization even faster, the mantra systems have special techniques revolving around deity yoga. The main technique is for a single consciousness to contain the two factors of observing a maṇḍala of deities and simultaneously realizing their emptiness of inherent existence. In this way, the vast (the altruistic appearance of deities) and the profound (the realization of suchness) are complete in one consciousness. This practice, called deity yoga, brings about speedier progress to Buddhahood.

All four divisions of the Mantra Vehicle—Action, Performance, Yoga, and Highest Yoga Tantras—have this special technique for developing unified concentration and wisdom. The first three describe a mode of progressing on the spiritual path in terms of yogas with and without signs, these being yogas of the non-duality of the profound and the manifest. Meditative stabilization is achieved within taking—as the object of observation of meditation—the clear appearance of your own body as the body of a deity, as has been described above in the three meditative stabilizations in Yoga Tantra. Then, while observing your body visualized as a deity's body, you ascertain its absence of inherent existence, thus making a combination of manifestation in divine form and profound wisdom realizing the final nature of that body. Such profound realization and simultaneous divine appearance is the yoga of the non-duality of the profound and the manifest, and is the chief distinguishing feature of Mantra.

Imagination of a divine body, which is in the class of compassionately vast appearances, accumulates the collection of merit, and hence a mind of deity yoga fulfills the feature of altruistic method. Also, since this very same mind ascertains the emptiness of inherent existence of the divine body and so forth, the collection of wisdom is accumulated; thus the same mind of deity yoga fulfills the qualities of wisdom. Although method and wisdom are still separable conceptually, they are contained in the entity of one consciousness.

In developing this combination, initially calm abiding must be achieved. As mentioned above, in Yoga Tantra you begin with meditating on a coarser object, a divine body, and then switch to observing a subtle object, a tiny five-pointed vajra, which is first generated at the navel area or the heart and then is drawn up to the nose and contemplated standing at the tip of the nose. The minute size of the vajra, which at the largest is the size of a grain of sesame, aids in removing excitement, and its brightness and location help in removing laxity.

Contemplating such a tiny vajra at the tip of the nose as the object of observation, a yogi achieves calm abiding—single-pointed meditative stabilization not interrupted by even subtle laxity or subtle excitement—such that the object is seen clearly as if with the eyes. Then, on the basis of this deep state of concentration conjoined with physical and mental pliancy, you imagine the diffusion of many tiny vajras from the single vajra at the tip of the nose and then imagine gathering them back, again and again. First, they are seen as pervading the body; then you extend them throughout the area—a mile or two—then a hundred, then a thousand, then ten thousand, then a hundred thousand miles, finally filling the billion worlds of this world system. After that, you gather them back to the single vajra at the tip of the nose; then, at the end of the session this single vajra is withdrawn to the heart.

The best of practitioners can develop the full form of the meditative stabilization on a subtle object by spending just two months on the first part, stable and clear appearance of a tiny vajra, and one month on the second part, diffusion and gathering back of many tiny vajras.

A practice similar to this is done in Highest Yoga Tantra in the Guhyasamāja system; thus, the presentation here can be of great benefit in understanding many points in the *Guhyasamāja Tantra.* In this sense, even though the *Compendium of Principles Tantra* is not a Highest Yoga Tantra, it is called a root tantra for the *Guhyasamāja Tantra,* since its rites for deity generation, meditation on a subtle object, and so forth are foundationally similar.

3. Yoga Without Signs

In both the Perfection Vehicle and the Secret Mantra Vehicle in order to achieve knowledge-of-all-aspects it is necessary to have the full complement of training in a union of the means to achieve a Buddha's Form Bodies (the collection of merit) and the means to achieve a Buddha's Truth Body (the collection of wisdom)—a union of method and wisdom. In the Mantra Vehicle, as indicated above with regard to Yoga Tantra, all of the steps of the yoga with signs cultivating a Buddha's Form Body in deity meditation are preceded by meditating on emptiness; however, the yoga in which meditation on emptiness becomes the central emphasis is the yoga without signs, even though the appearance of deities and so forth is maintained except in direct cognition of emptiness.

In cultivating the yoga of signlessness you are meditating, as in the sūtra systems, on emptiness with respect to persons and phenomena; however, here you are considering *special* persons and phenomena—yourself as a divine figure and all directions filled with pure Buddha bodies, vajras, mantra letters, and lotuses. These special objects are taken as the substrata, or subjects, and their ultimate nature is being reflected upon. In this way, there is a decided difference in the substrata with respect to which emptiness is realized. You are meditating on the final reality of the body, vajra, or the like, which are designated in dependence on a pure basis of designation.

In this way, although the emptiness of inherent existence—the noumenon—is the same in the sūtra systems and in all four tantra sets of Secret Mantra, the substratum of the quality of emptiness differs. In Mantra you are mainly meditating on a substratum—a divine body, for instance—newly established for your mind, whereas in the Perfection Vehicle the substratum are, for the most part, phenomena established through the power of karma, and their emptiness is being meditated. In the Mantra Vehicle in addition to newly establishing the substratum in imagination, you first meditate on emptiness, and then use this awareness ascertaining emptiness as the basis from which a divine body, for instance, is caused to appear to your mind. Given that the appearance factor of a consciousness realizing emptiness is appearing as a deity and its emptiness is being meditated upon, the substratum here is a pure phenomenon.

To repeat: You yourself meditate on emptiness, whereupon your awareness realizing emptiness appears as a new divine body, within continuously meditating on its emptiness. Since, when you are set in meditative equipoise on emptiness, you develop the "pride" that this wisdom consciousness is a Buddha's Wisdom Truth Body, the substratum—the divine body that appears within having this wisdom consciousness basis of emanation and that appears as its sport—is, for your imagination, a pure phenomenon, having the nature of the wisdom realizing emptiness. In this way, in Mantra it is said that the substrata whose emptiness is being meditated is pure.

Thus though the emptiness of an impure phenomenon and the emptiness of a pure phenomenon are the same, there is a difference. What is the difference? The continuum of an impure substratum will later cease, not existing in Buddhahood, whereas a pure substratum's continuum of similar type will exist right through Buddhahood. Since the deity as whom you are imaginatively meditating yourself is a divine figure—Vairochana, for instance—that exists in the state of Buddhahood when all defilements have been abandoned, this substratum is, for your imagination, pure.

Hence, it is important when doing deity yoga to put great effort into:

- working at realizing emptiness as much as you can
- then imagining that the wisdom realizing emptiness appears itself as a compassionately directed divine body with a face, arms, and so forth
- and then taking this divine figure as the substratum and continuously meditating on its emptiness.

Meditating on Emptiness

In Sanskrit the letter *a* indicates a negative, which in the system common to the Perfection Vehicle and the Mantra Vehicle is taken to mean the mere elimination of an object of negation—inherent existence—with respect to all phenomena. In this way the letter *a* constitutes the whole text of the shortest Perfection of Wisdom Sūtra. In addition, in Highest Yoga Tantra the letter *a* indicates the fundamental innate mind of clear light.

As in the sūtra systems, meditation on emptiness begins with gaining a sense of the inherent existence of which phenomena are empty, for without understanding what is negated, you cannot understand its absence, emptiness. Shāntideva's *Engaging in the Bodhisattva Deeds* says:[a]

---

[a] IX.140; P5272, vol. 99, 260.4.5. The Sanskrit is: *kalpitaṃ bhāvamaspṛṣṭvā tadabhāvo na*

Without contacting the superimposed existent
Its non-existence is not apprehended.

Through carefully watching how you conceive your self, or "I," to be inherently established, you will determine that the "I" appears to be self-instituting without depending on the collection of the mental and physical aggregates, which are its basis of designation, or without depending on any of them individually, even though the "I" appears with those aggregates. Proper identification of this appearance is the first essential toward realizing selflessness—ascertaining the object of negation.

However, if you identify only a coarser object of negation, you will refute only that and will be incapable of damaging the apprehension of inherent existence, having fallen to an extreme of superimposition. If, however, you mistake the object of negation too broadly and hold that everything appearing to sense and mental consciousnesses is itself the object of negation, you will fall to an extreme of denying conventionalities, whereby you will be in great danger of falling to the extreme of annihilation.

The second essential in the process of realizing emptiness is to determine that if the "I" is inherently established, it must be established as either the same as or a different entity from the mental and physical aggregates. Except for those two choices there is no other way it could be established. Thus, the second step—the essential of ascertaining the entailment—is the determination that whatever is not established as either the same as or a different entity from its basis of designation is necessarily empty of inherent existence.

Then, you examine the two possibilities. If the self and the aggregates are one inherently established entity, they must be utterly indivisible. For if something is inherently existent, a contradiction between how it appears and how it is cannot occur, since the mode of being of that object would have to appear exactly as it is to any awareness to which it appears. Consequently, if the "I" and the mental and physical aggregates are inherently established as one, there are the faults that:

- Just as one person has many mental and physical aggregates—body and mind, for instance—so there would absurdly have to be many persons.
- Or, just as there is no more than one person, so the aggregates also would absurdly be one.

---

gṛhyate. See Vidhushekara Bhattacharya, ed., *Bodhicaryāvatāra,* Bibliotheca Indica vol. 280 (Calcutta: Asiatic Society, 1960), 221.

- Just as the mental and physical aggregates are produced and disintegrate, the person also would be inherently produced and would inherently disintegrate.

There are many such reasonings. Determination that the "I" and the mental and physical aggregates are not an inherently established unity through this kind of analysis is the third step—the essential of ascertaining the absence of being the same.

Then, you turn to analyzing whether the "I" and the mental and physical aggregates are inherently different. If they are, they must be factually other, unrelated objects that are different in all ways, such as in entity, substance, and so forth. Being merely conceptually different and not different from the viewpoint of entity is the sign of a falsity, and thus such is not possible in what is inherently established. For if the "I" and the mental and physical aggregates are unrelatedly different, then when the aggregates grow old, become sick, and are finally discarded, the "I" would not become sick, aged, and so forth. As a result, the "I" would absurdly not have the character of the aggregates, such as production and disintegration. Also, upon mentally eliminating the five aggregates a separate self would have to be demonstrable. In this way, the determination that the "I" and the mental and physical aggregates lack inherently established difference is the fourth step—the essential of ascertaining the absence of being plural.

From these ascertainments, you can conclude that the "I" does not inherently exist. For example, when a bull is lost and there are no more than two areas where it could have gone, if a person searches for it in those fields, merely seeing that it is not in those areas produces the clear thought, "The bull is not there." In the same way, once you have identified how the object of negation—here the inherently existent "I"—appears to a consciousness conceiving inherent existence, then when you keep an overly concrete sense of the object in mind and analyze whether it is one with or different from its basis of designation, at the conclusion of those reasonings, the "I" that was identified earlier as so concretely existing will disappear, and you will conclude that such a self does not exist. This is realization of the selflessness, the emptiness, of the "I." This same realization can be extended to all other phenomena, such as body, mind, mountain, house, tree, and so forth without any further reasoning, although there are many other modes of reasoning.

Though you cannot find these phenomena—or any of the exalted phenomena involved in cultivating deity yoga—under analysis, this does not mean that they do not exist conventionally. No phenomenon exists as its own reality, but this does not rule out nominal existence.

In both the yogas with and without signs you meditate on the emptiness of inherent existence of yourself as a deity, the deity in front, and so forth—reflecting on their sameness in suchness, which is just this elimination of inherent existence. In the yoga without signs, the appearance of yourself and the deity in front vanish in the face of the ascertainment factor of the wisdom realizing emptiness but continue to appear to the appearance factor of that same consciousness. The maṇḍala residence and divine residents—the substrata of the quality of emptiness of inherent existence—are to be viewed as the sport of the ultimate mind of enlightenment, a Bodhisattva's exalted wisdom realizing emptiness, a mere elimination of inherent existence just as space is the mere elimination of obstructive contact. This is Mantra's unique union of the profound (realization of emptiness) and manifestation (compassionate ideal form), an undifferentiable union of wisdom and method.

PROGRESS ON THE PATH

The speedy attainment of the path of seeing and concomitantly the wisdom of the first Bodhisattva ground is a unique imprint of these special practices. Through the yoga with signs you attain fully qualified calm abiding conjoined with physical and mental pliancy, and then through the yoga without signs you attain special insight—a state arisen from meditation within the category of analytical meditation that has emptiness as its object. Even though, in the process of achieving calm abiding, you have eliminated the laxity and excitement that would interfere with stabilizing meditation, here during the phase of alternating stabilizing meditation with analytical meditation there is another level of laxity and excitement that interfere with the development of special insight. The laxity and excitement that occur when analyzing are slightly different from those that occurred earlier during cultivation of calm abiding, and thus it is necessary again to pass through the four mental engagements—forcible, interrupted, uninterrupted engagement, and effortless engagement.

Here is how to alternate analytical and stabilizing meditation: After analyzing with individual investigation, desist from such analysis and set the mind single-pointedly on the meaning you have understood. However, before the mind becomes too settled, switch again to analytical meditation, alternating in this way between stabilizing and analytical meditation.

Gradually, the power of analysis itself will be able to induce physical and mental pliancy similar to those explained earlier with respect to calm abiding, but to a greater degree. Generation of a bliss of physical and mental pliancy, induced through the power of analysis, no longer requiring alternation between analytical and stabilizing meditation, marks the attainment of fully qualified special insight—and thereby the attainment of the path of preparation—and from this point on, you have a union of calm abiding and special insight. You now have powerful means for realizing the emptiness of inherent existence in order to overcome obstructions when it is brought to the level of direct perception.

Though specific tantras, or even specific passages in tantras, emphasize either stabilizing or analytical meditation, it is necessary to alternate these two equally until special insight is attained through the bliss of mental pliancy being induced not by the power of stabilizing meditation, but by the power of analysis itself. Therefore, it is not sufficient merely to withdraw the mind inside or even first to become mindful of the view of emptiness and then set merely in stabilizing meditation. Analysis is necessary. This is the thought of all three masters expert in Yoga Tantra—Shākyamitra, Buddhaguhya, and Ānandagarbha—who are the reliable sources for Yoga Tantra in India.

PURPOSE OF YOGAS WITH AND WITHOUT SIGNS

Cultivation of the yogas with and without signs constitute approximation—approaching closer to the deity. Approximation is not just a matter of reciting a certain number of a mantra but of cultivating these yogas in meditation, through which you advance on the path. Capacity must be developed. These practices mainly revolve around deity yoga and emptiness yoga. Without deity yoga, the special, profound features of tantra are absent, and without the view of emptiness you cannot develop an antidote to the afflictive obstructions and the obstructions to omniscience. Therefore, you must develop the imprint of these two practices for an approximation to be actual. You must know how to cultivate deity yoga—how to develop clear appearance of the deity and so forth in the context of the non-arising of the faults of laxity and excitement—and in particular you must know how to meditate on emptiness properly.

Without knowledge of these steps of the path, if you just memorize and recite the text of a rite, this does not constitute approximation. Also, the purpose of approximation is not just to make you ready to confer initiation on others or to consecrate images and so forth, but to develop the capacity of a steady, concentrated consciousness in order to analyze and penetrate the profound nature of phenomena—all for the sake of being of greater service to others.

Although the general mode of procedure is the same as in the sūtra system, the special objects and techniques of tantra make the achievement of a union of calm abiding and special insight—and consequently the first Bodhisattva ground and its direct realization of emptiness—much faster. With direct perception of emptiness, obstructions can gradually be removed completely and forever.

4. Feats

When you have attained mastery with respect to the general meditation—unified meditation on a divine circle and on suchness—and in particular with respect to the meditative stabilization on a subtle object, you engage in additional practices to achieve mundane and supramundane feats. The additional practices are of three types—concentration, repetition, and burnt offerings. Mundane feats are, for instance, to clairvoyantly reveal treasures such as mineral wealth under the ground. Supramundane feats here include the great seal [that is, an actual divine body], knowledge-fund of long life, and so forth.

Even during the process of initiation there are cases of students achieving the feat of revealing where treasure is, for instance. The lama has performed the full form of the approximation required for bestowing initiation, and the student has trained his or her continuum well through the paths common to the vehicles. Also, both the lama and the student have, with great concentration, recited the mantra of the descent of the wisdom-being [that is, the actual deity]. Then, when a lama with high realization bestows initiation on such a student with all the qualifications, the lama puts emphasis on the mantra for the descent of the wisdom-being, and upon its descent the student can reveal where treasure is, and so forth, merely by turning attention to that topic.

With respect to feats that are achieved through additional concentration after completing approximation, meditation is required until signs of success occur. Although deity yoga is a prerequisite for this process, Yoga Tantra masters disagree on whether the meditator as the pledge-being [that is, yourself imagined as a deity] should cause the wisdom-being [the actual deity] to enter yourself. In any case, the additional concentration is done within the context of visualizing yourself as a deity.

For instance, for the feat of revealing treasure, you meditate on a treasure-pot at your heart, inside which is a vajra on top of a moon—the vajra accords in color with your own lineage. Repeating the mantra *vajra-nidhi,* you meditate until a sense of being able to see and feel what is being visualized arises. Since you have already attained full qualification with respect to meditative stabilization, you would, most likely, only have to exert slight effort for these signs of success—a sense of being able to touch and see the visualized object—to arise. You then meditate for an entire evening, and then upon going to the general area where treasure is suspected to be, you make offerings and so forth, and again engage in meditation and repetition, whereby the treasure is seen.

It is said that Ḏzong-ka-ḇa himself did not pay much attention to material wealth, since he understood that in the future students would become distracted and thus hurt by too much external property. However, there is no question that one who has dexterity with meditative stabilization can reveal where gold and so forth are in the ground.

For feats of walking on water or in space, you meditate on the particles of water and air respectively as being hard like vajras. This causes the capacity of these particles to cover and block an area to become more manifest. Though in an ordinary state a coarse body cannot be supported by the subtler particles of water and air, through single-pointed meditation you are able to get down to that level and enhance their capacity for supporting even gross objects.

Buddhaguhya's *Introduction to the Meaning of the Tantra*[37] and its commentary by the master Padmavajra[38] describe how to achieve many different types of feats in considerable detail. These include achieving clairvoyance, love, compassion, the altruistic intention to become enlightened, and so forth. In Yoga Tantra there is also the achievement of an actual body that is a special type of form having the marks of a Buddha's body; this seems to be like the mental body achieved through the path of the Perfection Vehicle. The process is to generate yourself as the deity and then imagine that all of space is filled with similar small Buddha bodies, which are brightened with the exhalation of breath and drawn into your heart with the inhalation of breath, like butter melting into sand. By contemplating this again and again, capacity is gradually achieved, whereby eventually your body turns into a Bodhisattva Knowledge-Mantra Bearer who has a similitude of the form of a Buddha.

As explained above, in dependence on profound techniques of deity yoga and subtle objects of meditation you quickly achieve a meditative stabilization that is a union of calm abiding and special insight. Then, based on this, you first achieve common feats and then uncommon, or special, ones such as that of a Knowledge-Mantra Bearer. Through these, in turn, your progress on the path is enhanced.

The attainment of a union of calm abiding and special insight marks the beginning of the path of preparation, as this is the point of attaining a state arisen from meditation observing the emptiness of inherent existence.

Then, when this truth—the final nature of phenomena—is seen directly, you attain the path of seeing and the first of the ten Bodhisattva grounds. From there on, the remainder of the path ranging from passing to the path of meditation with the attainment of the second ground through the tenth ground is mostly similar to that of the Perfection Vehicle. This, in brief, is the mode of procedure on the path of Yoga Tantra.

II: The Great Exposition of Secret Mantra: Yoga Tantra

by Ḏzong-ka-ḇa

The Stages of the Path to a Conqueror and Pervasive Master, a Great Vajradhara: Revealing All Secret Topics[39]

Part Four, Stages of Progressing on the Path in Yoga Tantra

1. The Root Tantra

The presentation of the stages of the path in Yoga Tantra has two parts: how these are taught in the tantras and the stages of practicing the meaning of the tantras.

How the Stages of the Path Are Taught in Yoga Tantras

[The Parts of the Compendium of Principles Tantra]

The root of all Yoga Tantras is the *Compendium of Principles.*[40] The introduction at its beginning teaches about Vairochana, who possesses a fulfillment of the aims of both [oneself and others], thereby generating [in the listener] a wish to attain [the state of Vairochana]. All of the tantra from that point on indicates the means—once that wish has been generated—by which the object of attainment [the state of Vairochana] is actualized.

Concerning this, the shared[a] means of achieving mundane and supramundane feats are taught in the root tantra. Furthermore, it has four sections—the "Vajra Element," "Conquest over the Three Realms," "Taming Transmigrators," and "Achieving Aims" sections. The first [section teaches the paths of][41] the Vairochana lineage—the latter of the two [terms], One-Gone-Thus and One-Gone-Thus lineage, [being another name for] the Vairochana lineage.[b] The second [section teaches the paths] of the Akṣhobhya

---

a "Shared" means that the root tantra, in general, sets forth methods for all four lineages in common, whereas the individual sections of the root tantra stress certain lineages.

b Buddhaguhya (*Introduction to the Meaning of the Tantra, rgyud kyi don la 'jug pa, tantrārthāvatāra,* P3324, vol. 70, 67.3.5) also uses the terms *de bzhin gshegs pa* and *de bzhin gshegs pa'i rigs.* Ke-drup's *Fundamentals* (216.7) explains that the term "One-Gone-Thus" is used to refer to all five lineages, whereas the term "One-Gone-Thus lineage" is used to refer to the members of the Vairochana lineage and not those of the other four lineages. Seemingly, he goes on to say that the first section teaches the paths of both the One-Gone-Thus and the One-Gone-Thus lineages; however, no other text directly supports this position and thus the reading may be wrong, but it is supported indirectly by Ḏzong-ka-ḇa's mention below (71) of a "repeater of the One-Gone-Thus" which Ke-drup's *Fundamentals* (220.11) takes to mean the five Ones-Gone-Thus.

lineage—the vajra lineage; the third [section teaches the paths of] the Amitābha lineage—the lotus lineage; and the fourth [section teaches the paths of] the Ratnasambhava lineage—the jewel lineage fulfilling the wishes of sentient beings.

Buddhaguhya[42] explains the reason why the root tantra sets forth only four lineages despite there being five: [the last lineage] is the jewel lineage from the viewpoint of being the agent fulfilling the thoughts of sentient beings and is the action lineage from the viewpoint of being the activities of doing so; hence, action and agent have been condensed into one.

The Continuation of the *Compendium of Principles Tantra* takes care of [that is, was taught for the sake of] the best of the best sentient beings who [like the internal yoga of meditative stabilization and][43] achieve supramundane feats. It teaches features of the supreme feats that serve as causes for attaining Buddhahood and Bodhisattvahood. It also teaches paths related to all four sections [of the *Compendium of Principles* in the sense of expanding on them and filling in incomplete explanations].[44]

The Continuation of the Continuation of the *Compendium of Principles Tantra* was set forth as a means to take care of sentient beings who—because of not being able to understand the meaning of the principles, that is, the special methods for achieving the supreme feat—have apprehension,[a] are frightened by cultivation [of the internal meditative stabilization[45] of deity yoga], and are attached to [external][46] activities such as repetition [of mantra], offering, and so forth. It teaches paths [for achieving worldly feats][47] related to all four sections [in the sense of expanding on them and filling in incomplete explanations].[48] Despite [this part being taught for those frightened by cultivation of deity yoga] this does not contradict [the explanation that] Yoga Tantras were taught for trainees who mainly cultivate [deity yoga].[49] For it is not contradictory that although the chief trainees mainly cultivate [deity yoga], the secondary ones [such as those for whom the Continuation of the Continuation was taught] do not.[b]

---

[a] This likely means that they have apprehension of conventional factors imbued with a sense of inherent existence such that they cannot meditate well on emptiness.

[b] Ke-drup's *Fundamentals* (218.8-220.7) explains this point in more detail:

> *Question:* One of the two ways of positing the four tantra sets is that:
>
> - Those tantras set forth in terms of trainees who, between internal yoga and external activities such as bathing, cleanliness, and so forth, prefer external activities, are posited as Action Tantras.
> - Those tantras set forth in terms of trainees who prefer to engage equally in

[The Four Sections as Being Both for Separate Persons and for One Person]

Question: Are the paths of the four sections for persons of different continuums or are they four different states of a single person gradually being led [to higher states]?

Answer: Concerning this, Ānandagarbha's *Extensive Explanation of the "Shrīparamādya Tantra"*[50] says that:

- A repeater [or practitioner][51] of the [five][52] Ones-Gone-Thus has a good nature and engages [in the afflictive emotions of desire, hatred, obscuration, and miserliness][a] equally.
- A repeater of the One-Gone-Thus lineage [that is, a trainee of the first section] is desirous.
- A trainee of the second section is hateful.
- A trainee of the third is obscured or has wrong views.

---

both external activities and internal yoga are posited as Performance Tantras.

- Those tantras set forth in terms of trainees who, between these two, prefer the internal yoga of meditative stabilization, are posited as Yoga Tantras.
- Those tantras set forth in terms of trainees who prefer the internal yoga with respect to which there is none higher are posited as Highest Yoga Tantras.

Is there a contradiction between this explanation and the one that the Continuation of the Continuation of the Yoga Tantra [that is, of the *Compendium of Principles*] was set forth for trainees who like external activities?

Answer: For example, with respect to the trainees of the *Guhyasamāja Tantra* [in the Highest Yoga class] there are two types of special trainees—(1) supreme trainees, jewel-like persons who even though they have completed the stage of generation do not seek common feats but seek to attain the supreme feat upon practicing the stage of completion and (2) secondary trainees, such as those like a white lotus who, upon completing the stage of generation, seek common feats, the eight great feats, and so forth. Just as there are these two types of trainees among the four lineages [of practitioners, the latter three lineages being in the second category], so the special trainees of Yoga Tantra are also of two types—main and secondary. The explanation [that Yoga Tantras were spoken for those who like internal yoga] is in terms of the main trainees from between these two types and not the secondary. Hence, there is no fallacy."

This way of positing the four tantra sets is explained in H.H. the Dalai Lama, Tsong-ka-pa, and Jeffrey Hopkins, *Tantra in Tibet,* 162-164. Another way involving four different ways of using desire in the path is explained in *Tantra in Tibet,* 156-162.

[a] Ke-drup's *Fundamentals* (220.11) speaks of the three poisons—desire, hatred, and obscuration—which I take to be an abridgement of the four.

- A trainee of the fourth is miserly.

Therefore, [according to this explanation the paths of the four sections are for] persons of different continuums. This is like the explanation in Highest Yoga Tantra of the mantra repeaters of the five One-Gone-Thus lineages [in which it is said that a desirous person can gain achievement more easily by depending on Amitābha, that a person who tends towards hatred can do so in dependence on Akṣhobhya, and so forth].[a]

However, from the viewpoint of object of attainment, that same commentary associates the four lineages—One-Gone-Thus, vajra, lotus, and jewel/action,[b] respectively, with the Four Bodies (Nature, Fruition, Complete Enjoyment, and Emanation) and the four exalted wisdoms (mirror-like, equality, individual realization, and achieving activities) as well as with the mind of enlightenment, the perfection of giving, the perfection of wisdom, and the perfection of effort. When treated this way, [the paths of] all four lineages [or, in other words, the paths of all four sections] are necessary for the objects of attainment of each trainee [since all trainees must achieve the Four Bodies as well as the mind of enlightenment and the perfections. Therefore, each of the four lineages of trainees come to be trainees of all four sections.][53]

[Seventy-Two Meditative Stabilizations]

With respect to actualizing the state of Vairochana, in each of the four sections [of the *Compendium of Principles Tantra*] three sets each of meditative stabilizations [called initial preparation, supreme royal maṇḍala, and supreme royal activities][54] are described for trainees who like extensive, middling, and brief [paths] (see chart, 45). The four sets of three middling meditative stabilizations [initial preparation, supreme royal maṇḍala, and supreme royal activities] are [the three meditative stabilizations][55] explained at the point of the four-seal maṇḍala[c] in the respective [sections].[56] The four

---

[a] See the Dalai Lama's commentary, 29.

[b] The order of these in Ḏzong-ka-ḇa's text (One-Gone-Thus, vajra, jewel, lotus, and action, which accords with the names of the deities around the central figure) has been emended to accord with the order of the Four Bodies and so forth with which they are correlated in the rest of the sentence. Ḏzong-ka-ḇa also uses the original order (One-Gone-Thus, vajra, jewel, lotus, and action) in the section on cultivating subtle yoga.

[c] The central figure in the four-mudrā maṇḍalas is one of the five Buddhas, who is surrounded by the other four Buddhas in the form of mudrās (and hence the name "four-mudrā

sets of three brief meditative stabilizations are [the three meditative stabilizations][57] explained at the point of the single-seal maṇḍala[a] in the respective [sections]. With respect to the four sets of three extensive meditative stabilizations, three meditative stabilizations each—initial preparation, supreme royal maṇḍala, and supreme royal activities—are described in the individual [four] sections at the point of the great maṇḍala, retention maṇḍala, doctrine maṇḍala, and action maṇḍala. [Thus, each section describes four complete ways to actualize the extensive form of the three meditative stabilizations].[58]

[Four Sections, Lineages, Mandalas, Bases of Purification, Afflictive Emotions, Seals, and Effects of Purification]

The correlation of the four lineages and four seals in the four sections [of the *Compendium of Principles Tantra*] in Ānandagarbha's *Illumination of the Principles* is a correlation of the four—exalted body, mind, speech,[b] and activities—with the four lineages of the sections, since the great seal is exalted body, the pledge seal is exalted mind, the doctrine seal is exalted speech, and the action seal is exalted activity. Buddhaguhya's *Introduction to the Meaning of the Tantra*[c] extensively explains this together with proofs [beginning with the passage]:[59]

> By way of the features of exalted body and so forth seals also are taught here as of four types—that called the "great seal," and the pledge, doctrine, and action seals.

The exalted body and so forth that are correlated in this way are cases of treating the lineages of Vairochana, Akṣhobhya, Amitābha, and the other

---

maṇḍala"). There are five four-mudrā maṇḍalas in each of the four sections of the *Compendium of Principles*, with each of the Buddhas of the five families at the center of his own four-mudrā maṇḍala, surrounded by a distinctive set of four mudrās (vajras, lotuses, hooks, and so forth). (Thanks to Steven Weinberger for the note.)

a The single-mudrā maṇḍalas consist of a single deity on a moon-disc in the center of the maṇḍala. (Thanks to Steven Weinberger for the note.)

b The text reads "body, speech, mind, and activities"; the order has been altered in translation to accord with the order of the four sections in the *Compendium of Principles Tantra* and with the rest of the sentence.

c As here (147.7), Ḏzong-ka-b̄a frequently refers to Buddhaguhya's text by the Sanskrit *avatāra*.

two lineages [Ratnasambhava and Amoghasiddhi] as exalted body, mind, speech, and activity [respectively] and not cases of treating the exalted body and so forth of any one deity [as those four, even though each deity has all four—exalted body and so forth].

[However, this is not the only way that these groups of four are correlated, for] Ānandagarbha also speaks in his *Illumination of the Principles*[60] within the context of correlating the great, retention, doctrine, and action maṇḍalas of **each** of the four lineages with the four seals. Hence, he does this in terms of all four—exalted body, mind, speech, and activity—in each lineage [not just correlating one among exalted body, mind, speech, and activity with each lineage]. Also Buddhaguhya's *Introduction to the Meaning of the Tantra* says:[61]

> In [each of] the four lineages the great maṇḍala is to be viewed as being an abbreviated emanation of the treasury of inexhaustible exalted body because the deities set [there] are configurations of Form Bodies. The pledge maṇḍala[a] is an abbreviated emanation of the treasury of configurations of inexhaustible exalted mind [in the form] of symbols which are set [there as] vajras, hooks, arrows, snapping fingers,[b] and so forth symbolizing the door of release [that is, the non-conceptual wisdom] as it is to be realized. The doctrine maṇḍala is the magnificently blessed emanation of the treasury of configurations of the inexhaustible exalted speech of all Ones-Gone-Thus—deities set [there] abiding in the equipoised activity of methods teaching the doctrine as it is to be realized. Likewise, since deities of actions such as offering and so forth are arrayed in the action maṇḍala, it is to be viewed as displaying—in abbreviated form—the activities of all Ones-Gone-Thus for the welfare of sentient beings, and so forth.

Furthermore, since Ānandagarbha's *Illumination of the Principles* speaks from the viewpoint of predominance, in the first maṇḍala of the Vajra Element section, for instance, the great seal of exalted body of its own lineage is predominant, but it is not that the pledge seal of exalted mind and so forth

---

a *dam tshig gi dkyil 'khor*, which is also called retention maṇḍala (*gzungs dkyil*).

b According to the Dalai Lama, of the sixteen Sattvas, Vajrasattva's hand-symbol is a five-pointed vajra; Dor-jay-gyel-ba's (Vajrarāja) hand-symbol is a vajra hook; Dor-jay-chak-ba's (Vajrarāga) hand-symbol is an arrow; and Dor-jay-lek-ba's (Vajrasādhu) hand-symbol is snapping fingers (*mgu ba*).

are absent. Hence, seal-impression with [all] four seals is also set forth [in the Vajra Element section]. The same also should be understood for the other [sections].[a] In this vein, Buddhaguhya's *Introduction to the Meaning of the Tantra* says:[62]

> Through these stages the four maṇḍalas are set forth, since the four aspects of exalted body and so forth are predominant [in the respective sections and within the respective maṇḍalas within the sections]. However, since there mostly is no mind without body and no speech without mind and body, it should be seen that all four—exalted body and so forth—are required in the individual maṇḍalas. Therefore, those which have the character of exalted body and so forth—respectively the great seal as well as pledge, doctrine, and action seals—are set forth here [in the tantra] also for all the maṇḍalas of the lineages.

If you know these distinctions in detail, you will understand the non-contradiction of the explanations in Ānandagarbha's *Extensive Explanation of the "Shrīparamādya Tantra"* of the paths of the four sections sometimes within combining them as factors in the full enlightenment of one person and sometimes as paths of persons with separate continuums.

There are frequent descriptions in Yoga Tantra of causing the wisdom-being [that is, the actual deity] to enter into yourself generated as a deity and of seal-impression by way of the four seals.[63] These are methods of attaining the four seals of the fruit [state as a Buddha] through transforming the four—body, speech, mind, and activities—into divine body, speech, mind, and activities, and thereby purifying ordinary body, speech, mind, and activities (see chart, 32).

Although in this way stages of the path based on individual lineages are frequently described, the repeater of mantra of the "One-Gone-Thus lineage" or "Vajradhara lineage" is supreme. One who has been conferred the complete initiation [of a master] in a maṇḍala of the Vajra Element is a

---

[a] Ke-drup's *Fundamentals* (226.1-226.6) elaborates:

> Furthermore, although Vairochana is mainly body, it is not that speech, mind, and activity are absent; hence, there is seal-impression with the four seals. Also, although Akṣhobhya is mainly mind, he has body, speech, and activity. Also, although Amitābha is speech, he has body, mind, and activity. Also, although the other two lineages [Ratnasambhava and Amoghasiddhi] are mainly activity, they have body, speech, and mind. Hence, there is seal-impression with the four seals.

master of all lineages, whereas those of the other lineages are partial masters. Ānandagarbha establishes this with sources in his commentary on the first part of the *Compendium of Principles.*

[PATTERN OF DEITY YOGA]

Question: Then are the paths that are to be cultivated as methods for actualizing Vairochana just the three meditative stabilizations?

Answer: The path is not complete with just those, for prior to them you must also cultivate the great yoga, the path of self-completion[a] [which is a special deity yoga involving meditation of many deities].[64]

Cultivation of deity yoga in the pattern of the stages of production of [a life] in cyclic existence [mimicking the process of death, intermediate state, and rebirth]—the thoroughly afflicted class [of phenomena]—is not set forth in any reliable text of the three lower tantra sets; consequently, such is a distinguishing feature of Highest Yoga Tantra. However, [in the three lower tantra sets] there is a cultivation of deity yoga in the pattern of the very pure class [of phenomena], for the cultivation of the five manifest enlightenments[b] [in Yoga Tantra, for instance] is said to be meditation within assuming the pride of such-and-such [stage] in accordance with the stages of full purification of Bodhisattvas in their last lifetime. Therefore, even though with respect to cultivation of the paths prior to [the cultivation of the five manifest enlightenments] the three masters [Buddhaguhya, Shākyamitra, and Ānandagarbha] do not—except for a mere mention in Ānandagarbha's *Illumination of the Principles*—set forth a correlation [of those stages of the path] individually with the four paths [of accumulation, preparation, seeing, and meditation], it is clear that buddhafication by way of the five manifest enlightenments and [the paths] before it are meditations in the pattern of a learner's paths [in that they are patterned after the stages of enlightenment of Bodhisattvas in their last lifetime and before]. Also, [it is

---

[a] The answer may be a criticism of Bu-ḋön's *Condensed General Presentation of the Tantra Sets, Key Opening the Door to the Precious Treasury of Tantra Sets* (*rgyud sde spyi'i rnam par gzhag pa rgyud sde thams cad kyi gsang ba gsal bar byed pa*), in Collected Works, vol. 14, 881.7, where Bu-ḋön says that the main methods are the three meditative stabilizations. On 87 below, Ḍzong-ka-ḃa puts Bu-ḋön's source quote in context.

[b] For detailed descriptions of the five manifest enlightenments see below 123ff. and 154ff.

clear that] the paths [ranging from meditating on yourself as] having been buddhafied as Vairochana and after are meditations that accord with the deeds of one who has already become a Buddha.[65]

2. Initiation and Vows

STAGES OF PRACTICING THE MEANING OF THE YOGA TANTRAS

This section has four parts: (1) how to become a receptacle suitable for cultivating the path, (2) having become a receptacle, how to maintain purity of pledges and vows, (3) how to perform prior approximation while abiding in the pledges, and (4) how to achieve feats once the approximation is serviceable.

HOW TO BECOME A RECEPTACLE SUITABLE FOR CULTIVATING THE PATHS

You are made into a vessel suitable for cultivating the path and so forth through entering a maṇḍala such as that of the Vajra Element, receiving initiation, and receiving the pledges and vows. Concerning this, there are two types: those who merely enter a maṇḍala and those who enter [and receive initiation], of which there are two types. The former are those who cannot hold the vows of the five lineages but who hold the Bodhisattva vows; only the initiation of a student is granted to them. However, to those who can hold both [Bodhisattva and mantra] vows the full initiation of a vajra master is granted. Since I have discussed at length the presentation of such topics [in accordance with] the thought of Ānandagarbha's *Rite of the Vajra Element Great Maṇḍala: Source of All Vajras*[a] and Ānandagarbha's commentary on the first part of the *Compendium of Principles Tantra* in my *Explanation of the Root Infractions,*[66] I will not elaborate on them here.

[a] *rdo rje dbyings kyi dkyil 'khor chen po'i cho ga rdo rje thams cad 'byung ba, vajradhātumahāmaṇḍalopāyikasarvavajrodaya;* P3339, vol. 74; Toh. 2516, vol. *ku,* 43a-44a. This text is often referred to as *rdo rje thams cad 'byung ba* (*sarvavajrodaya*) or *rdo rje 'byung ba* (*vajrodaya*). Bu-dön has an extensive, very clear commentary on this text called *Extensive Explanation of (Ānandagarbha's) "Source of All Vajras": Wish-Granting Jewel* (*rdo rje thams cad 'byung ba'i rgya cher bshad pa yid bzhin nor bu*), in Collected Works, vol. 11, 185-832. It is in addition to *Practice of (Ānandagarbha's) "Rite of the Vajra Element [Great] Maṇḍala: Source of All Vajras": Wish-Fulfilling Jewel* (*rdo rje dbyings kyi dkyil 'khor gyi cho ga rdo rje thams cad 'byung ba zhes bya ba'i lag len rin chen bsam 'phel*), which, it might be said, is his Tibetanization of the translation of Ānandagarbha's text.

HAVING BECOME A RECEPTACLE, HOW TO MAINTAIN PURITY OF PLEDGES AND VOWS

At the beginning, it is indispensable to maintain purity of the pledges and vows taken after gaining initiation. Therefore, you should work at it without loosening your effort. Buddhaguhya's *Introduction to the Meaning of the Tantra* says:[67]

> Then those who have pleased the guru are bestowed initiation, in accordance with the rite, in a great maṇḍala or a pledge, doctrine, or action maṇḍala revealed by a guru. They take vows through the rite of clearly realizing the Great Vehicle[a] and become skilled in the pledges, discipline, deeds, and conduct to be thoroughly kept. For the sake of henceforth keeping the pledges and so forth as promised, they should never loosen their enthusiasm, since keeping them precedes the complete achievement of the aims of yourself and others. Furthermore, at this point those who wish for the fruit [of practice] do not transgress the pledges. Thereby, deeds of body, speech, and mind concordant with pleasing your special deity and having the nature of engaging in virtue and disengaging from non-virtue, and so forth,[b] are the features of the way spoken by the teacher [Buddha].

The pledges and particularly the root infractions set forth in the *Shrīparamādya Tantra*[68] and the *Vajrashekhara Tantra*[69] are discussed at length in my *Explanation of the Root Infractions;* therefore, I will not elaborate on them here.

If the characteristics of keeping the pledges and so forth are not complete, [feats] will not be achieved. The *Vajrashekhara Tantra* says:[70]

> Though making effort
> Over hundreds of eons
> Four persons will not succeed
> Despite working at it in the world.
>
> Those who have not generated the altruistic intention

---

[a] According to Lati Rin-bo-chay, this perhaps refers to "the rite by which one becomes a person of the Great Vehicle," this being the rite for taking the Bodhisattva vows.

[b] The Dalai Lama suggested that "and so forth" indicates that finally one gives up even neutral states, manifesting only virtue.

To become enlightened, those with doubt,
Those not acting according to the word,
And the faithless will not succeed.

Since it says that those who have [any of] the four faults will not achieve [yogic feats] despite striving over many eons, you should possess four advantageous qualities:[a]

1. training, in accordance with the quintessential instructions, in the altruistic intention to become enlightened—the door of entry to the Great Vehicle—and thereby generating it with all its characteristics
2. having great conviction in tantra and thereby not having doubt and two-mindedness
3. having the ability to keep pledges in the way they are explained—the trainings of engagement [in virtue] and disengagement [from non-virtue] formulated by the Conqueror [Buddha]
4. having firm faith in the deity and guru.

Thus, a practitioner should practice within abiding in the vows of a householder or a monastic. The *Vajrashekhara Tantra* says:[b]

Dwelling in a householder's vow
Abandoning killing, stealing,
Sex,[c] lying, and intoxicants,
You then achieve the knowledge monarch.

---

[a] Ḏzong-ka-ḇa expands here on material similar to that in Bu-d̄ön's *Condensed General Presentation of the Tantra Sets,* in Collected Works, vol. 14, 881.1.

[b] D480, vol. *nya,* 199b.4-199b.5. This is cited in Buddhaguhya's *Introduction to the Meaning of the Tantra* (P3324, vol. 70, 50.2.8-50.3.1); the translation in the Peking edition is slightly different:

> */gsod dang rku dang 'khrig pa dang/ /rdzun dang chang ni rnam par spang/ /khyim pa'i tshul du gnas nas ni/ /rig sngags rgyal po rtag par bsgrub/ /gal te de ni rab byung na/ /sdom pa gsum la gnas par bya/ /so sor thar dang byang chub chen/ /rig 'dzin rang gi sdom pa'o/*

The Peking reading justifies my treatment of the syntax when translating it into English.

Like Ḏzong-ka-ḇa's citation, the second stanza of the tantra (D480, vol. *nya,* 199b.4-199b.5) reads:

> *gal te de ni rab byung gyur/ /sdom pa gsum la yang dag gnas/ /so sor thar dang byang chub sems/ /rig 'dzin sdom pa mchog yin no/*

[c] *'khrigs pa;* for householders with vows of pure behavior this refers to sex in general, whereas for others it refers to adultery.

If you leave the household and truly abide
In the three vows—individual liberation,
Bodhisattva, and Knowledge Bearer[a]—
It is supreme.

Householders, if they are suitable to be a basis for [a vow of] individual liberation, also should practice within having come to possess the three vows.

[a] That is, a tantric practitioner.

3. Observing a Deity

HOW TO PERFORM PRIOR APPROXIMATION WHILE ABIDING IN THE PLEDGES

This section has two parts: yogas with and without signs.

Yoga With Signs

This section has two parts: the yoga of four sessions observing the coarse, a deity; and the yoga of four sessions observing the subtle, a hand-symbol.

Yoga of Four Sessions Observing the Coarse, a Deity

This section has two parts: cultivation in four sessions and the procedure for those unable to do so.

Cultivation of the Yoga Observing the Coarse, a Deity, in Four Sessions

This section has two parts: the yoga of four sessions for those who have obtained only a student's initiation and for those who have obtained a master's initiation.

Yoga of Four Sessions for Those Who Have Obtained Only a Student's Initiation

The explanation of two different paths in terms of a master and a student in Ānandagarbha's commentary on the first part of the *Compendium of Principles*[a] refers to two levels, one in terms of those who have obtained a master's initiation and one in terms of those who have obtained only a student's initiation.

With regard to the mode of meditation by those who have obtained only a student's initiation, Ānandagarbha's commentary on the first part of the *Compendium of Principles* says:[71]

---

[a] The reference here is to two types of paths explained in Ānandagarbha's commentary on the first part of the *Compendium of Principles;* it is not in reference to the two *Means of Achievement* by him, both of which are from the viewpoint of a student's path.

> Concerning the student type, you should know about blessing yourself and so forth in the following way. Having performed self-protection, bathing with water, and again self-protection and place-protection, make a request to your deity to be seated in front [of yourself]. Make obeisance, disclose ill-deeds, admire [your own and others'] merit, make entreaty, supplication, and dedication, generate the altruistic intention to become enlightened, go for refuge to the Three [Jewels], and so forth. Having constructed the vajra-palms and vajra-binding,[a] open the vajra-palms at the heart, and make firm the descent of the vajra [that is, the wisdom-being].[72] Then meditate on selflessness, and, as before, meditate on a moon disc and so forth:[73] construct the great seal [that is, the physical form] of your own deity just as it should be. Causing the wisdom-being [that is, the actual deity] to enter in the proper way, practice achievement of the great seal. Then saying *jaḥ hūṃ baṃ*[b] *hoḥ,* with application of mental goodness cause all the Ones-Gone-Thus to enter your own body. Having thoroughly activated [that divine body] by way of your pledge seals, do seal-impression with the seals of your own deity, all Ones-Gone-Thus, doctrine, action, and the great seal. Bless yourself into magnificence with the pledge seal of the lineage. Confer initiation with the initiation of your own lineage, and then thoroughly make offering with the four secret offerings by the Goddess of Charm and so forth.[c] Having made obeisance to all the Ones-Gone-Thus, meditate well on your own great seal [that is, the divine body]. Repeat your deity's mantra—*vajrasattva* and so forth. Meditate in four sessions every day for a year.

Accordingly, having first bathed, perform the yoga of ferocity and create a protective circle. Then, bow down in the presence of [the beings that are] the basis for the accumulation [of merit] and go for refuge, and so forth. Then, make [the seals—that is, hand gestures—] ranging from the vajra-

---

a For these two hand-configurations, see seals 5 and 6.

b Or "*vaṃ.*"

c Vajralāsye, Vajramāle, Vajragīte, and Vajranṛtye. Buddhaguhya's *Introduction to the Meaning of the Tantra* (P3324, vol. 70, 42.5.2-42.5.3) says: *rdo rje lāsye la sogs pa gsang ba'i mchod pa rnam pa bzhis.* (Thanks to Steven Weinberger for the note.)

palms through the descent of the wisdom-being. Through the five rites[a] generate yourself as whoever your deity is; cause the wisdom-being who is similar to [the deity as whom] you [are imagining yourself] to enter, and perform seal-impression with the four seals.[b]

Then perform seal-impression with the four seals[c] on [your divine body which] limitless Ones-Gone-Thus have been caused to enter. Bless yourself with [the pledge seal of] the lineage; confer initiation on yourself with whatever the initiation of the lineage is; perform worship with offerings; and make obeisance. Then, meditate on the great seal of exalted body, and repeat the [mantra] of the specific deity. Except for the single yoga [of the one deity] there is no great yoga [in which many deities are meditated].

Meditation of an inestimable mansion is also not described [in Ānandagarbha's commentary on the first part of the *Compendium of Principles*. However] both the longer and shorter *Means of Achievement Called "Source of Vajrasattva"*[74] by Ānandagarbha explain that at the end of the single Vajrasattva yoga you are set in space, and a lion seat is imagined in the middle of an inestimable mansion on Mount Meru on a series of stacked up elements, onto which [yourself as Vajrasattva] descends from space and sits. Concerning this, Ānandagarbha's longer *Means of Achievement Called "Source of Vajrasattva"* explains:[75]

> Having [said] "*vajradhātu*" and constructed the seal of the supreme enlightenment, generate yourself as Vairochana. Saying "*vajrasattva*," emanate a Vajrasattva from your heart, setting him also on a lion seat contemplated in front [of yourself]. Then reciting Vajrasattva's essence[-mantra] and constructing his great seal, contemplate yourself as Vajrasattva.
>
> Further, from the letter *hūṃ* [at the heart] emanate Hūṃkara, and saying the mantra and making the seal of opening doors, mentally open the four doors. Then with the mantra and seal of

---

a For detailed descriptions of the five manifest enlightenments see 123ff. and 154ff. See also Bu-ḏön's *Extensive Explanation of (Ānandagarbha's) "Source of All Vajras": Wish-Granting Jewel*, in Collected Works, vol. 11, 334.5.

b Ke-drup's *Fundamentals* discusses the four seals expansively, whereas Ḏzong-ka-ḇa mentions them only in passing; for Ke-drup's exposition see 128ff.

c As examples of the four seals, see those of Vajrasattva (seals 1-4). The doctrine seal of Vajrasattva that is depicted there is for those mainly performing yoga without signs, which is the hand-configuration of meditative equipoise. The doctrine seal of Vajrasattva for those mainly performing yoga with signs is the same as the great seal of Vajrasattva.

> gathering the vajra [deities], gather the Buddhas.[76] Meditating on them as Vajrasattvas, praise them with the hundred names. Having drawn in [the wisdom-beings] and caused them to enter and so forth with the mantra and seal of the four doorkeepers, make seal-impression with the four seals. At the end of the offering, meditate on the three equalities[a] and do repetition [of mantra].

Ānandagarbha's shorter *Means of Achievement*[77] explains that having descended from space, you emanate a Vajrasattva on a second lion seat contemplated in front. It does not mention meditation of yourself as Vairochana [but the longer *Means of Achievement*[78] does].

Thus, since Ānandagarbha's commentary on the first part of the *Illumination of the Principles*[79] describes single yoga for students and the great yoga for masters, it is clear that the single yoga explained in his two *Means of Achievement* is done in terms of students. Even though in his *Illumination* he does not mention meditation on an inestimable mansion or a deity in its center or in front, since he does describe these in his two *Means of Achievement,* these are required even for students.

The explanation in the two *Means of Achievement* to meditate on yourself as Vajrasattva is to be taken as an exemplification of the flower-hit [when dropping a petal from above onto a maṇḍala divided into quadrants to determine the lineage of the deity as whom you will do self-generation], which should be done in accordance with the statement in his *Illumination* to meditate on yourself as whatever your deity is.[b]

If you wish to perform the yoga of the four sessions through these ritual stages, it is sufficient to take Ānandagarbha's commentary on the first part of the *Illumination of the Principles* as your basis and do it in accordance with what appears in either the longer or shorter *Means of Achievement Called "Source of Vajrasattva."* Since they are easy to understand and I fear it would run to too many words, I will not elaborate on them. I will explain below (87) the degree of yoga that is to be generated in meditation.

---

[a] As the Dalai Lama (38) says, this is to view (1) yourself, (2) all sentient beings, and (3) all the deities of the maṇḍala as equally without self, that is to say, inherent existence.

[b] As the Dalai Lama says (44), Vairochana/Vajrasattva is the main deity in the first section, "Vajra Element"; Hūṃkara is the main deity in the second, "Conquest over the Three Realms"; Amitābha is the main deity in the third, "Taming Transmigrators"; Amoghasiddhi is the main deity in the fourth, "Achieving Aims."

Yoga of Four Sessions for Those Who Have Obtained a Master's Initiation

With regard to those who have obtained a master's initiation there are two [situations to explain]. From between them:

1. If they wish to bestow initiation on a student, they must—as described in Ānandagarbha's *Rite of the Vajra Element Great Maṇḍala: Source of All Vajras*—perform the great yoga of self-completion[a] and do either:
   - an extensive divine approximation cultivating, without any abbreviation, the three meditative stabilizations,
   - a middling divine approximation, which is the abbreviated generation rite and so forth of the supreme royal maṇḍala, or
   - a brief divine approximation, which is comprised of the great yoga together with a hundred thousand repetitions for each deity [of the maṇḍala].
2. If they wish to achieve their own deity, Ānandagarbha says that the great yoga must be performed even for achieving their own deity. His commentary on the first part of the *Illumination of the Principles* says:[80]

   > Having thus explained yoga of your students [which involves self-generation through the five rites] and subsequent yoga [which involves entry of the wisdom-being, seal-impression, and consideration of yourself to be undifferentiable from the deity],[81] I will describe the rites of the great yoga for achieving a master's maṇḍala and achieving [a master's] own deity.

   Also, Ānandagarbha's longer *Means of Achievement Called "Source of Vajrasattva"* says,[82] "One who has attained a master's initiation should perform the great yoga and complete all the rites." Hence, he asserts that one who has fully obtained initiation must meditate on the basic deities in complete form, and he asserts that one who has not fully obtained initiation is not fit to meditate on the deities in complete form [since a student's initiation is limited to the single yoga of meditating on a single basic deity].

   Furthermore, merely the great yoga is not sufficient; the three meditative stabilizations must be cultivated because:

---

[a] *bdag rdzogs chen po'i rnal 'byor.*

- Ānandagarbha's commentary on the first part of the *Illumination of the Principles* says,[83] "Concerning that, I will explain the divisions of the method. Meditative stabilization is the actual method."
- Meditative stabilizations are divided into three—initial preparation, supreme royal maṇḍala, and supreme royal activities.
- Also, the three meditative stabilizations are set forth even with respect to the single-seal maṇḍala [that is, one deity] which is for those lowest [practitioners] who prefer a brief path.

and because the actual methods for actualizing Vairochana are said to be the three meditative stabilizations. Consequently, even if you cannot cultivate the three meditative stabilizations in extensive or middling form, you must cultivate the three brief meditative stabilizations as well as the great yoga. The great yoga does not have extensive, middling, and brief forms.[a]

With respect to the period of meditation, Ānandagarbha's *Rite of the Vajra Element Great Maṇḍala: Source of All Vajras*[84] speaks of meditating for a year, six months, or one month. Due to people being [of varying faculties]—best, middling, and least—the period is not definite as a single length. With respect to conferring initiation [on others], it is said that you should perform [the rite] until obtaining permission from the deities.

With respect to doing meditation until clear realization is generated, Ānandagarbha's commentary on the first part of the *Illumination of the Principles* says,[85] "Meditate every day in that way until the Vajra Element Great Maṇḍala is manifestly seen." Hence, in four sessions—in the morning, noon, afternoon and evening, and midnight[b]—you should stop the mind from being distracted to anything other than the stages of the rite as described, and without letting the stages of meditation pass as mere verbiage invoke generic images [that is, mental images] at each point. This should be sustained within analyzing [the status of phenomena] with the wisdom of individual investigation, whereby obstructors are overcome. A firm mind to

[a] Nevertheless, as Bu-dön's *Extensive Explanation of (Ānandagarbha's) "Source of All Vajras": Wish-Granting Jewel* indicates, there are more and less elaborate ways of performing the great yoga.

[b] According to Lati Rin-bo-chay, it is generally said that one should avoid having meditative sessions at sunrise, noon, sunset, and midnight; thus, these four may refer to general periods of time.

hold the pledges and vows [should be maintained], and your continuum should be purified through obeisance, offering, repetition, and so forth. Also, when doing the visualization of whatsoever deity yoga, you should meditate until clear appearance like that of direct perception arises. That is taken as the measure of having **initially** generated the yoga in the continuum; it is not that further meditation is not needed. This is the same for both master and student.

In the context of these [topics], achievement of the factor of stability in which the mind remains firmly on one object of observation is not clear[ly presented in the texts of these three masters]. This is in consideration of its being achieved [during the subsequent practice] of observing a tiny vajra. [That this is so can] be known from the part [in the *Compendium of Principles Tantra*][86] teaching its benefits [see 91ff.].

Since the great yoga of self-completion also is clear in its ritual formulation in Ānandagarbha's *Rite of the Vajra Element Great Maṇḍala: Source of All Vajras,* and since I fear it would run to too many words, I will not write about it.

The master Buddhaguhya does not differentiate individual stages of cultivating the path from the viewpoint of whether or not initiation is complete or whether you are conferring initiation on another or achieving your own deity. He indicates two modes of meditation by persons who have been conferred initiation in the Vajra Element Great Maṇḍala and possess the pledges and vows—one of a [pledge] being of the Ones-Gone-Thus and one of a [pledge][a] being of the One-Gone-Thus lineage. For whichever of these two is cultivated he describes no more than a single deity for each [that is, no other deities]. He describes meditation on a deity in front in an immeasurable mansion with a seat in accordance with the part on the Great Maṇḍala. For those who cannot do this he describes meditation on a deity in accordance with the parts on the four-seal [maṇḍala][87] and the single-seal [maṇḍala][88] and then keeping vows, external and inner offerings, praising, and so forth in four sessions. His system appears to be easier to perform than that of the master Ānandagarbha.

---

[a] Buddhaguhya's *Introduction to the Meaning of the Tantra,* P3324, vol. 70, 42.5.4-42.5.5: *de bzhin gshegs pa'i dam tshig gi sems dpa' chen po sgrub pa'i rnal 'byor* and *de bzhin gshegs pa'i rigs kyi dam tshig gi sems dpa' chen po sgrub pa.*

Procedure for Those Unable to Cultivate the Yoga Observing a Deity in Four Sessions[89]

Those who are unable to meditate on a deity through generating themselves as a One-Gone-Thus by way of the five manifest enlightenments in that way, and so forth, repeat only the essence-mantra of whoever the deity is and meditate on themselves as that deity [that is, consider themselves to be the deity but without clear imagination of such]. Also, having meditated on such a deity in front [in the sense of merely considering that the deity is present, without clear imagination], they make offering, praise, and so forth and then complete [the prescribed count] of mantra repetition. Buddhaguhya's *Introduction to the Meaning of the Tantra* says:[90]

> This means: Māntrikas who cannot perform the yoga of the pledge-being of their own deity as described merely repeat mantra. Also, through the meaning of that [essence-mantra] they consider themselves to be blessed into magnificence [as] the divine being whose mantra is being repeated, to be granted initiation, and to be endowed with meditative stabilization[a] and offering. Also, meditating on such [a deity] in front, they repeat mantra.

Furthermore, this generation of yourself as a deity solely through the words of the deity's essence-mantra is for those who are unable to meditate and want feats from mere repetition and so forth. Buddhaguhya explains, with sources from the [*Compendium of Principles*] *Tantra*, that such is not to be done if you can meditate. His *Introduction to the Meaning of the Tantra*[91] clearly explains this:

> This second way of establishing yourself as a pledge-being solely through the words of the meaning of the essence-mantra is taught for those who want feats from mere repetition. It is not for those who can practice through cultivating the great seal [of exalted body] and so forth. How is this? The Continuation of the Continuation of the *Compendium of Principles Tantra* at the point [of describing this] says at length:[92]
>
> > This secrecy is not fit
> > For those of bad views without desire.

---

[a] The Go-mang scholar Ḏen-ḇa-ḏen-dzin suggested that this might refer to clear appearance and cultivation of divine pride.

and so forth. Then it says:

> At the least, you transform yourself into the body of a Buddha through the meaning of the essence-mantra. You also meditate on a Buddha-body in front through mere words and perform repetition with the vajra words a hundred and eight times, since you wish [to do it] that way.

This is like designating the verbal convention "meditation" to the recitation of the ritual formulation of a deity yoga. Since even [such recitation] makes a great difference, those who perform the conferral of initiation on the living and on the deceased,[a] consecrations [of images], and so forth by way of Yoga Tantra must at least perform merely this meditation and do the respective complete repetition.

---

[a] According to Lati Rin-ḇo-chay, initiation of the deceased is done through summoning the person from the intermediate state to the previous body and then bestowing initiation.

4. Observing a Hand-Symbol

Yoga of Four Sessions Observing the Subtle, a Hand-Symbol

This section has three parts: (1) the purpose of meditating on a subtle object, (2) making the mind stable through observing a subtle object, and (3) how to perform diffusion, gathering, and so forth once stability is attained.

Purpose of Meditating on a Subtle Object

The first section of the *Compendium of Principles Tantra* says:[a]

> Then[b] set very much in equipoise,
> All objects of meditation
> Whatsoever will become stable.
> They appear[c] through the exalted wisdom of meditative stabilization.

[Commenting on this stanza] Ānandagarbha's *Illumination of the Principles* says[93] that once meditative stabilization of a subtle [or tiny] object is established, you are set in meditative equipoise, whereupon all [objects] to be meditated—the divine body and so forth—will become stable, that is to say, will become manifest. Hence, through this [observation of a subtle object] a special serviceability of mind is attained, enhancing everything that is meditated.

Moreover, Buddhaguhya's *Introduction to the Meaning of the Tantra* says that this [observation of a subtle object] definitely must precede achieving many feats by way of mere concentration, which will be explained later (110ff.):[94]

> Therefore, in particular, a yogi who wants feats arising from meditative stabilization must initially meditate on a subtle vajra.

---

[a] Stanza 457; Sanskrit in Kanjin Horiuchi, *Sarva-Tathāgata-Tattva-Saṃgrahaṃ Nāma Mahā-yāna-sūtra* (Wakayama-ken Kōya-chō: Mikkyō Bunka Kenkyūjo, 1983), 262: *tataḥ prabhṛti yat kiṃcid bhāvayet susamāhitaḥ / sarvaṃ caitad dṛḍhīkuryāt samādhijñānakalpitam //;* D479, vol. *nya,* 41a.6. This passage is cited in Buddhaguhya's *Introduction to the Meaning of the Tantra* (P3324, vol. 70, 52.1.2); the translations differ in minor ways.

[b] That is, after successfully cultivating the yoga observing a tiny object.

[c] *brtags pa.*

In brief, since this [practice] establishes a special calm abiding, the purposes of calm abiding are its purposes also.

Making the Mind Stable through Observing a Subtle Object

Buddhaguhya asserts that you meditate on a subtle object after deity yoga. His *Introduction to the Meaning of the Tantra* says:[95]

> In that way through [either of] the two forms—extensive or brief[a]—you should perform self-blessing as the pledge-being of your deity, conferral of initiation [on yourself, cultivation of] meditative stabilization, and offering. Then, initially for the time being, cultivate the meditative stabilization of a subtle vajra in order to gain control over your mind.

With regard to the stages of meditation, the first section [of the *Compendium of Principles*] says:[b]

> Having put the tongue to the palate,
> Concentrate on [a tiny vajra at] the tip of the nose.
> Through the blissful touch of the subtle vajra
> The mind will be set in equipoise.

The first two lines indicate techniques of placing [the body and mind], and the latter two indicate how placing [body and mind] that way generates meditative stabilization. As Buddhaguhya's *Introduction to the Meaning of the Tantra*[c] says, this is to be cultivated within mindfulness of your deity yoga.

With respect to the physical essentials, you should act in accordance with the statement in Shākyamitra's *Ornament of Kosala*[d] to finish all

---

[a] See 88.

[b] Stanza 454; Horiuchi, *Tattva-Saṃgrahaṃ*, 262: *jihvāṃ tālugatāṃ kṛtvā nāsikā'graṃ tu cintayet / sūkṣmavajrasukhasparśād bhavec cittaṃ samāhitam //;* D479, vol. *nya*, 41a.5. The passage is cited in Buddhaguhya's *Introduction to the Meaning of the Tantra* (P3324, vol. 70, 52.1.8); the translations differ in minor ways.

[c] Buddhaguhya's *Introduction to the Meaning of the Tantra*, P3324, vol. 70, 52.1.8-52.2.1: *rdo rje phra mo'i ting nge 'dzin gyi rim pa yang 'di ste/ dang por re zhig rang gi lha'i sems dpar bdag nyid ji ltar bsgrubs pa rjes su dran par byas.*

[d] *de kho na nyid bsdus pa'i rgya cher bshad pa ko sa la'i rgyan, tattvasaṃgrahaṭīkākosalālaṃkāra;* P3326, vols. 70-71; Toh. 2503, vol. *yi*, 154a.7-154b.2. According to the Go-mang scholar Ḍen-ḅa-ḍen-dzin, Kosala is one of six famous cities in India. Tāranātha says

activities, stay in an isolated place that is not noisy, straighten the body in a cross-legged posture, put the tongue from its root upward behind the upper teeth, and put the two lips together. You should also possess the other forms of behavior for meditative stabilization.[a] Then place the color and so forth of the subtle vajra, which is the object of observation to be meditated, at the tip of the nose in just the way you have ascertained it [through looking at a vajra or picture of it] and hold the mind on it.

Moreover, Buddhaguhya's *Introduction to the Meaning of the Tantra*[96] describes the vajra as five-pointed, like the color of your deity, and ranging in size from the most subtle, just the tip of a hair, to the largest, just a sesame seed. Ānandagarbha[97] asserts that at first it should be generated at the navel, and then upon saying *sukṣmavajra*[b] it is drawn up from there and, [emerging] from the nose, is to be contemplated as standing at the tip of the nose.[c] Shākyamitra[98] asserts it as rising from the heart. Padmavajra's *Commentarial Explanation of (Buddhaguhya's) "Introduction to the Meaning of the Tantra"*[d] explains that while mentally reciting the essence-mantra[e] it is drawn with the movement of wind [that is, breath] from the heart to the tip of the nose.

Buddhaguhya[99] explains that when meditating within observing a subtle vajra, if you stop the exhalation and inhalation of wind [that is, breath] and

---

Shākyamitra was from Kosala, this being how the text gets its name. A.K. Warder's *Indian Buddhism* frequently mentions Kosala, a territory adjacent to Magadha along the Ganges.

[a] The recommended posture has seven features:

1. sit on a cushion in the vajra or half-vajra posture
2. keep the eyes partly closed and aimed at the tip of the nose
3. keep the body and spine straight
4. keep the shoulders level
5. keep the head even, bent a little down, the nose in line with the navel
6. set the teeth normally, with the tongue against the ridge behind the upper teeth
7. breathe quietly and gently.

[b] Buddhaguhya's *Introduction to the Meaning of the Tantra* (P3324, vol. 70, 52.2.3) identifies *oṃ sukṣmavajra* as the essence-mantra of the subtle vajra.

[c] Although there are other meditations in other contexts on objects at the point between the brows, here the object is standing upright (*'greng ste gnas pa*) at the tip of the nose.

[d] *rgyud kyi don la 'jug pa'i 'grel bshad, tantrārthāvatāravyākhyāna;* P3325, vol. 70; Toh. 2502, vol. *'i,* 242a.5. The Otani catalogue of the *sde dge* edition at Tohoku gives the author's name as Padmavajra; the Peking edition (and catalogue) gives the author as Vajra; Dzong-ka-ba cites his name as Gel-sang-dor-jay (*skal bzang rdo rje*).

[e] This is likely the essence-mantra of the subtle vajra, *oṃ sukṣmavajra.*

hold it at the nose, a special sense of touch[a] concordant with the mind's abiding [stably] is generated. With regard to the way to hold the mind, Shākyamitra[100] cites Bhāvaviveka's *Heart of the Middle* and says to do it that way:[101]

> The crazy elephant of the mind behaving wildly
> Is tied to the pillar of an object of observation
> With the rope of mindfulness.
> By degrees it is brought under control with the hook of wisdom.

"Wisdom" here is introspection.[b] Hence, the example of taming an elephant indicates the achievement of a serviceable mind by way of the two—mindfulness and introspection. The subtle vajra that is the base on which the mind is being set is like a stable pillar to which an elephant is tied. The unserviceable mind is like an untamed elephant. Causing the mind not to be distracted from its object of observation through relying on mindfulness is like using a rope to tie an elephant. Setting [the mind] free from fault—when it does not hold the object of observation as [originally] set—through immediately recognizing such by means of introspection is like a herder's hitting an elephant with a hook and correcting it when it strays from the tie-up.

Hence, there are two important factors with regard to holding the mind:

- From the beginning, stay on the object of observation without being distracted to anything other than it.
- Then if distracted, immediately recognize such, and again focus [the mind] as before.

Concerning this, since the first depends on sustaining undistracted mindfulness, you should initially visualize the object of observation, and by generating a strong mode of apprehension [or intentionality] thinking, "[My mind] is set in such and such a way," do not be distracted. Since a mode of sustaining mindfulness that has not developed force in the mind cannot eliminate laxity, Shākyamitra's *Ornament of Kosala* says,[102] "Establish mindfulness with clear and non-lethargic awareness."

The second factor depends on the mode of sustaining introspection. Therefore, having tied [the mind to its object of observation] with

---

a Literally, "object of touch," something pleasant to feel.

b *shes bzhin, saṃprajanya.*

mindfulness, at intervals not too far apart nor too close you should inspect whether or not the mind is remaining [on the object] in accordance with how it was tied, again and again merely looking into it without losing stability.[a]

Concerning this, it is said that if [the mind] is too tight, excitement is generated, and if too loose, laxity is generated; therefore, you should come to know [through your own experience] the area free from those. When, through sustaining this, the subtle vajra becomes stable, bliss will be generated at the tip of the nose or in another place in the body. This is generation of physical pliancy, a special object of touch capable of clearing away the assumption of bad physical states and so forth involving unserviceability of the body—the body's being unfit to be directed to virtuous activities. Becoming free from assumption of bad physical states, the body is serviceable, due to which you can make intense effort. Physical pliancy generates mental pliancy, for as it is said, "Physical pliancy experiences bliss, and through being blissful the mind becomes single-pointed."[b]

In this way Shākyamitra's *Ornament of Kosala*[103] clearly sets forth the mode of generating calm abiding, endowed with a single-pointed mind, based on a subtle object of observation. [His explanation] does not contradict the description in Asaṅga's Treatises on the Grounds[104] that mental pliancy generates physical pliancy, which in turn generates calm abiding. For it can be known from the sūtra Shākyamitra cites as a source that in his [explanation] mental pliancy is asserted to be the calm abiding of single-pointedness [and not the mental pliancy generated prior to calm abiding to which Asaṅga refers].

It is clear that you train in this [observation of a subtle vajra] until calm abiding is established, since [observation of a subtle vajra] is developed until physical and mental pliancies are generated. Moreover, first you should train until good, clear appearance of the deity is gained and then, when cultivating this [observation of a subtle vajra], you should meditate continuously for two months, dividing [the day] into four sessions. Ānandagarbha's commentary on the first part of the *Compendium of Principles Tantra* says,[105]

---

[a] If checking to see whether you are distracted is done too frequently, this itself will promote distraction.

[b] For a thorough presentation of how to achieve calm abiding, see Gedün Lodrö, *Calm Abiding and Special Insight,* trans. and ed. by Jeffrey Hopkins (Ithaca: Snow Lion, 1998), Part One, and for the pliancies, 97-116.

"If you meditate for two months in four sessions each day, the signs [of success] will definitely be attained."

How to Perform Diffusion, Gathering, and so forth Once Stability Is Attained

The first section of the *Compendium of Principles Tantra* says:[a]

> When the sign of blissful touch
> Of the subtle vajra arises,
> Wherever the sign is extended
> The mind is to be extended.
>
> Extending the mind as you wish,
> Extend it even through the three realms.

Ānandagarbha's commentary on the first part of the *Compendium of Principles* says[106] that when, through the force of having meditated on the form of the subtle vajra, your body is seen as entirely pervaded [by tiny vajras], then if you wish to increase [the sphere of the vajras], you diffuse them through the town, and so forth, and then through the three realms.

With respect to how to diffuse [the tiny vajras], Buddhaguhya's *Introduction to the Meaning of the Tantra*[107] explains that saying[b] *spharavajra* ["diffuse vajras"],[c] you scatter many vajras like a whirlwind blowing on dust, whereby they become pervasive by degrees. Having done contemplation in that way for a long time, say *saṃharaṇavajra*[108] ["gather vajras"], and while experiencing the touch of withdrawing wind [that is, breath,] inside, withdraw the vajras to the tip of the nose, whereupon they become one vajra,

---

[a] Stanzas 455, 456ab; Horiuchi, *Tattva-Saṃgraham*, 262: *sūkṣmavajrasukhasparśa-nimittaṃ jāyate yadā / sphārayet tan nimittaṃ tu tac cittaṃ sarvataḥ spharet // yathecchāspharaṇāc cittaṃ traidhātukam api spharet /;* D479, vol. *nya*, 41a.6: *rdo rje phra mo'i bde reg ba'i/ /mtshan ma gal te byung ba dang / /mtshan ma de ni khyab bya ba/ /sems ni kun tu khyab par bya/ /ji tsam 'dod par sems khyab nas/ /khams gsum du yang* ***khyab*** *par 'gyur/.* This passage is cited by Buddhaguhya, P3324, vol. 70, 52.2.6-.7. In his citation, the last two lines read: *ji ltar 'dod par sems spros pa/ /khams gsum yang ni* ***khub*** *par bya/.*

[b] Buddhaguhya (P3324, vol. 70, 52.2.2, 52.2.4, 52.2.7, and 52.3.1) says that these are to be mentally spoken.

[c] The Peking edition of Buddhaguhya's text (P3324, vol. 70, 52.2.7) reads *sparavajra.*

and meditate on it. The first section of the *Compendium of Principles Tantra* says:[a]

> Then upon having gathered them back,
> It dwells at the tip of the nose.

Shākyamitra's *Ornament of Kosala* explains[109] that it then enters the right nostril and, placed at the heart, is made stable. Do so saying *oṃ dṛḍhatiṣṭha*[110] ("*oṃ* stand firm").

This training in dexterity with respect to a variety of diffusions and withdrawals after first seeking and establishing calm abiding observing a subtle object is a special cause of mental serviceability. Therefore, its power is not the same as sustaining only a dwelling [of the mind in one way]. Ānandagarbha's commentary on the first part of the *Compendium of Principles* explains[111] that if you meditate for three months—[the two months mentioned above as well as] one month on diffusion and what comes after it,[b] meditative stabilization on a subtle object [can be] completed.

When understanding forms with respect to this extensive explanation of the subtle yoga in the *Compendium of Principles* and its commentaries, it appears to make a great difference with regard to many topics concerning the [practices called] clear realizations[c] of the *Guhyasamāja Tantra*[112] as commented upon by the Superior [Nāgārjuna] and so forth, [such as] with regard to initial establishment of the factor of stability and then, once it is established, training in dexterity.

---

[a] Stanza 456cd; Horiuchi, *Tattva-Saṃgrahaṃ*, 262: *punas tu saṃharet tat tu yāvan nāsāgram āgatam //;* D479, vol. *nya,* 41a.6. This passage is cited by Buddhaguhya, *Introduction to the Meaning of the Tantra,* P3324, vol. 70, 52.2.8.

[b] "Diffusion and what comes after it" refers to the repeated practice of diffusion and gathering.

[c] *mngon rtogs, abhisamaya.*

5. Yoga Without Signs

Yoga Without Signs

This section has three parts: (1) how yoga without signs is explained in the *Compendium of Principles,* (2) how yoga without signs is explained in an explanatory tantra, and (3) a brief exposition of how to cultivate it.

How Yoga Without Signs Is Explained in the Compendium of Principles Tantra[113]

The *Compendium of Principles* says:[114]

> Through understanding the letter *a*
> All letters are thoroughly meditated.
> When meditating from your own mouth
> And in the other's mouth, feats will be attained.
>
> This called "penetrating wisdom"
> Is renowned as meditative stabilization.
> Through it a seal will be achieved.
> If meditated, you will quickly achieve.
>
> Wisdom is meditative stabilization
> [Without][115] following the tones and spreading to the words.
> If you meditate with it,
> Feats of secret-mantra will be quickly gained.
>
> The features of secret-mantra
> And knowledge-mantra do not differ.
> Through cultivating wisdom
> Feats will be quickly gained.

Buddhaguhya's *Introduction to the Meaning of the Tantra*[116] explains that even though the term "essence" does not occur in the first stanza, the four stanzas [refer to] cultivating the wisdom realizing suchness respectively in terms of essence[-mantra], seal[-mantra], secret-mantra, and knowledge-mantra.

Concerning this, it is said that "Since *a* is non-produced, it is the door of all phenomena." Hence, through entering into [that is, through understanding] the meaning of *a* as the absence of inherently existent production, you are to meditate by way of the reasoning proving that all the mantra letters to be repeated lack a self of phenomena. Having been broken down, they do not appear.

"Mouth" is equivalent to "entry" and "door"; therefore, it [means] "your own entry and the other's entry." Through entering into the meaning of *a,* you enter into non-appearance, and then the other—the deity in front—enters into non-appearance.

If the meaning of "mouth" is taken as "door," then since the divine bodies meditated—yourself and in front—are the doors for release, they are called the "doors of self and other." Entering into those two [means the same] as before [that is, their disappearing]. This passage mainly indicates the investigatory wisdom that passes in steps from one to the other, the deities—yourself and in front—and the mantra letters, individually analyzing them as not established as [their own] suchness.

[With respect to the second stanza][117] penetrating wisdom observes the ultimate, and since it is said to be "meditative stabilization," analytical investigation has been stopped, and [the mind] is set a little in equipoise. The third [wisdom, mentioned in the third stanza] also has the word "meditative stabilization," and [the wisdom mentioned in] the fourth [stanza] is indicated as not different from it. Consequently, Buddhaguhya's *Introduction to the Meaning of the Tantra*[118] says that masters explain that the latter three [stanzas] predominantly, or chiefly, teach calm abiding. Though two predominances with respect to analytical and stabilizing meditation are indicated [the former being stressed in the first stanza and the latter in the other three], both must be performed equally in practice.[119]

[With respect to the third stanza, meditation][120] setting single-pointedly—without investigation continuing from one [thought] to another, following after and spreading to the tones of the mantra letters—is meditative cultivation of the wisdom of secret-mantra.[a] [With respect to the fourth stanza,][121] knowledge-mantra is said to be similar to secret-mantra. [This means that] the different appearances of the [individual] letters of a secret-mantra or of a knowledge-mantra are to be made non-different through reasoning analyzing them to be without inherent existence.

Though all four [wisdoms] are similar with regard to meditating on the

---

[a] Here "secret-mantra" refers to one of the four types of mantra and not the Secret Mantra Vehicle, which is equivalent to "Tantra".

meaning of settling that the deities—yourself and in front—as well as the mantras repeated are without inherent existence, the cultivations of the wisdoms of essence[-mantra], seal[-mantra], secret-mantra, and knowledge-mantra are differentiated. This is done in terms of how the repeaters of the four lineages—the One-Gone-Thus, vajra, lotus, and action lineages—meditate. I will explain this [in the next section].[a]

How Yoga Without Signs Is Described in an Explanatory Tantra

This section has four parts: how yoga without signs is cultivated in the One-Gone-Thus, vajra, jewel, and lotus lineages.

How Yoga Without Signs Is Cultivated in the One-Gone-Thus Lineage[122]

Meditate on yourself as [having] a body of a Buddha such as Vairochana, and contemplate the letters of the mantra at the heart of similar deities meditated in front [filling space].[b] Then, delineate the selflessness of persons and phenomena with respect to the deities—yourself and in front. When ascertainment of their absence of inherent existence is gained, meditate single-pointedly [on emptiness] through the meditative stabilization of the non-appearance of forms and so forth as separate. The *Vajrashekhara Tantra* says:[123]

> Repeaters of the One-Gone-Thus lineage
> Dwell auspiciously with the nature of a Buddha.
> They meditate [also] on Buddha bodies [in front
> Filling] these billion worlds.
>
> Meditate on the letters of your mantra

---

[a] This paragraph is not in Buddhaguhya's *Introduction to the Meaning of the Tantra.* Since, except for knowledge-mantra, in the next section Ḏzong-ka-ḇa does not mention essence-mantra, seal-mantra, or secret-mantra, it seems to me that his discussion of the four lineages implicitly covers essence-mantra, seal-mantra, and secret-mantra due to the fact that these four are correlated with the four lineages.

[b] From the subsequent meditations, it seems to me that the meditation is not on just one set of deities (yourself and a deity in front) but on many deities that pervade space; however, Buddhaguhya does not mention such. It also could be that the meditation is on two Buddhas—yourself and a deity in front—as large as a world system of a billion worlds.

At the heart of those Buddhas.
[Contemplate] your body as selfless,
Empty [of a self] of persons and phenomena.

Also contemplate the bodies
Of those Buddhas as selfless.
What is this Buddha form?
Its inherent existence does not exist.

A Buddha who is an [inherently existent] "person" does not exist.
[A Buddha] is not the aggregates and constituents.
There is no [inherently existent] Buddha [within] subject and ob-
ject.
Buddhas are not [conventionally] non-existent either.

Having thoroughly purified with wisdom
The seeds of the six perfections,
A yogi without a place for the basis-of-all[a]
Apprehends suchness, enlightenment, selflessness.

If those of the One-Gone-Thus lineage do repetition
With a yoga such as this,
The Very Joyful[b] will be achieved
Sooner than a great eon.

How Yoga Without Signs Is Cultivated in the Vajra Lineage[124]

[Meditate] on yourself as Vajrasattva and place the mantra letters in the center of the forms of vajras that are contemplated in front of yourself as filling the sky. Then, when ascertainment of the absence of inherent existence is gained through individually taking apart form and so forth, set [your mind] single-pointedly on that [emptiness] and meditate. The *Vajrashekhara Tantra* says:[125]

Then repeaters of the vajra lineage
Make themselves into Vajrasattva.

---

[a] Perhaps the "basis of all" is a consciousness conceiving inherent existence.

[b] If "Very Joyful" is taken as referring to the first Bodhisattva ground, it accords with the position, presented by the Dalai Lama in his introduction to *Tantra in Tibet,* that the feature of greater speed in the three lower tantras is that the period up to the first ground is faster. Otherwise, "Very Joyful" could be taken as referring to Buddhahood.

They meditate [also] on vajra forms
[Filling] these billion worlds.

Meditate on the letters of knowledge-mantra
In the center of those vajras.
The vajras also are a fruit of the mind
Of enlightenment [realizing] the absence of inherent existence.

What is this called "vajra"?
Suchness that is immutable.
What is this called "suchness?"
Emptiness that is called reality.

Meditate on all phenomena
In the aspect of emptiness.
When forms are broken down into particles,
This called a "particle" does not [inherently] exist.

Forms are called "empty."
That [emptiness] is called "vajra."
By means of such yoga
The Very Joyful is quickly achieved.

How Yoga Without Signs Is Cultivated in the Jewel Lineage[126]

[Meditate] on yourself as Vajraratnasambhava, and contemplate mantra letters in space in front of yourself. Then, when ascertainment with respect to the meaning of delineating object and subject equally as not truly existent is gained, meditate on that [emptiness] single-pointedly. The *Vajrashekhara Tantra* says:[127]

Then repeaters of the jewel lineage
[Make themselves] into Vajraratnasambhava.
They meditate on these billion worlds
In the aspect of emptiness.

The yogi contemplates in that space
The knowledge-mantra letters.
This called the absence of inherent existence of phenomena
Is called emptiness, thusness.

Forms assigned as internal

And external are not [inherently] produced.
Where form does not [inherently] exist
How could it be said the eye does?

Because form and eye do not [inherently] exist,
Consciousness does not [inherently] arise.
As it is with the eye, so it is with all.
[Inherently existent] object and subject are thoroughly abandoned.

This mode of yoga is the supreme
For achieving the Very Joyful.

How Yoga Without Signs Is Cultivated in the Lotus Lineage[128]

[Meditate] on yourself as Lokeshvara, and set the mantra letters on lotuses contemplated in front of yourself as filling the sky. Then, when ascertainment with respect to the meaning of delineating all phenomena as not inherently existent is gained, meditate on that. The *Vajrashekhara Tantra* says:[129]

Then repeaters of the lotus lineage
Make themselves into Padmasattva.
They should thoroughly meditate
On these billion worlds in the form of lotuses.

They meditate on knowledge-mantra letters
On those great pure lotuses.
They thoroughly contemplate the essence of phenomena
Through skill [arising] from [contemplating] those lotuses.

Just as a lotus is not sullied by water
Nor affected by the faults of mud,
So all phenomena are pure. The basic element
Of phenomena[a] is from the start not produced.

What is this matrix-of-One-Gone-Thus?
The empty noumenon of phenomena
Is called the "noumenal thusness"
Of all phenomena—forms and so forth.

Through the mode of this yoga,

---

a *chos dbyings, dharmadhātu.* I translated this also as "element of attributes."

Great yoga with great asceticism,
You are buddhafied in this very life,
Definitely achieving Padma[sattvahood].

Familiarizing again and again with these is designated with the name "repetition," but it is not repetition of mantra syllables.[a] Buddhaguhya's *Introduction to the Meaning of the Tantra,* after describing repetition with observation, says:[130]

> For those intelligent yogis who know the selflessness of phenomena I will explain the yoga of ultimate wisdom—the other features of repetition taught in the *Compendium of Principles* and the *Vajrashekhara.*

These have been stated [here] in accordance with Buddhaguhya's explanation [of the yoga without signs] in which he quotes statements from the *Compendium of Principles* and the explanatory tantra [the *Vajrashekhara*].

Brief Exposition of How to Cultivate Yoga Without Signs

What the *Vajrashekhara* describes is mainly special insight sustained through analysis by the wisdom of individual investigation, whereas the statements in the *Compendium of Principles* have both special insight and calm abiding—analyzing and setting [the mind] without analyzing. Also, Shākyamitra's *Ornament of Kosala* describes the character of calm abiding and special insight in this way:[131]

> Calm abiding has the character of contemplation within meditative stabilization; it is a mind operating on a single object of observation. Special insight is wisdom; moreover, it has the character of a mental factor of thorough analysis of phenomena. It has the aspect of differentiating with a mind of equipoise, "This is contaminated; that is uncontaminated. This is thoroughly afflicted; that is very pure."

Calling the individual differentiation of the contaminated, uncontaminated, and so forth special insight [refers to] the special insight observing the varieties [of phenomena]; through its illustration the special insight observing

---

[a] This sentence is not in Buddhaguhya's *Introduction to the Meaning of the Tantra.* The reason behind Ḏzong-ka-ḇa's mentioning that this is not repetition of mantra syllables is that Buddhaguhya calls such meditation "repetition"; see the following quotation.

the mode [of being of phenomena, that is, emptiness] should be known.

If only the stabilizing meditation of calm abiding is done, you finally become lax and lethargic. If only the analytical meditation of special insight is done, you finally become excited. Hence, calm abiding and special insight are to be cultivated equally. Excitement is cleared away by taking to mind an object of observation generating sobriety, such as impermanence. Laxity and lethargy are cleared away by taking to mind an object of observation that heightens [the mind] such as great luminosity appearing to the mind.

Shākyamitra's *Ornament of Kosala* says that when—through doing such—a natural equal operation [of calm abiding and special insight] without the activity [of applying the antidotes to laxity and excitement] is attained, that is a union [of calm abiding and special insight]:[132]

> If calm abiding predominates, the mind tends to the distraction of lethargy, whereas if special insight predominates, the mind tends to the distraction of excitement. Therefore, overcoming the two factors of distraction through respectively taking brightness to mind and taking impermanence to mind, you should dwell [with calm abiding and special insight] in unison on the thing being contemplated. Unison [means] to turn your awareness, like a horse, away from the deterioration of calm abiding or special insight—whichever it is—with the rein of mindfulness, and thereupon to join it to the right way. This means that [a mind] having the nature of operating with this aspect by way of a unison [of calm abiding and special insight] operates without the activity [of applying the antidotes to laxity and excitement].

Buddhaguhya asserts that when meditating on emptiness, you should do it in conjunction with the wind yoga of stopping vitality and exertion [that is, stopping breath and distraction]. His *Introduction to the Meaning of the Tantra* says:[133]

> Make manifest a belief in the emptiness of all phenomena by way of meditating on what is being contemplated—yourself, the deity, and the letters to be repeated—as not [inherently] produced. Internally, stop the two, vitality and exertion [that is, breath and distraction] which are the bases [of the movement] of the mind, and with a mind free from the appearance of forms and so forth consider yourself, the deity, and the letters being repeated as like space.

He explains[134] that when exhaling, the breath should be let out within experiencing the touch of subtle wind [that is, fine breath] inside the nose and that the deity in front should be recollected [at that time]. He says that again [upon inhaling] you should—as before—stop vitality and exertion [breath and distraction] and do [the contemplation of emptiness without the appearance of any form.

Some, on the other hand,] assert that merely setting the mind in non-conceptuality without holding it on anything and without settling the meaning of selflessness by way of the view is the yoga of meditating on the suchness of things. Others assert that the generation of a blissful, clear, non-conceptual meditative stabilization through the force of wind yoga and so forth is the yoga of meditating on the suchness of things. [However, these are contradicted by the above explanations of how to meditate on emptiness; hence] these assertions are not even the system of the three lower tantra sets, not to mention Highest Yoga Tantra. Also, [some hold that] during meditation you should not sustain ascertainment of the view through calling it to mind despite having [previously] delineated the meaning of selflessness through the view but should sustain a mere setting of the mind in general without conceptualizing anything. [However,] this is not meditation on the meaning of suchness. Therefore, you who want liberation, know unerringly how to seek the view of selflessness and how to meditate on its meaning once it is found.

The master Ānandagarbha again and again sets forth here and there in his great commentaries on the *Compendium of Principles* and the *Shrīparamādya* the delineation of the view and its great importance. Also, in his [longer] *Means of Achievement Called "Source of Vajrasattva"*[135] he sets forth mere seeds of the meditation of the three equalities at the end of deity meditation. However, he does not explain the modes of meditating on emptiness [as found] in the *Compendium of Principles* and the explanatory tantra [the *Vajrashekhara*] in one continuous discourse as does Buddhaguhya. Also, he does not describe the individual characters of calm abiding and special insight, the faults of the predominance of the one or the other, and the mode of their union as does Shākyamitra. Nevertheless, with respect to how to meditate on emptiness as explained above, the three masters expert in Yoga Tantra [Buddhaguhya, Shākyamitra, and Ānandagarbha] have the same thought. Consequently, you should hold onto the essentials of how, through the thought of Yoga Tantra, to generate meditative stabilization with signs—sustaining deity yoga and subtle yoga in four sessions—and how then to generate meditative stabilization of signlessness as explained above.

The meaning of prior approximation[a] described here [under the topics of yogas with and without signs] is to approach closer to the object of attainment.[b] The Continuation of the *Guhyasamāja Tantra* says:[136]

> Approximation is asserted as twofold
> Through the division of common and supreme.

Just as it describes both the methods for achieving the two feats [common and supreme] as approximations, so it is here [in Yoga Tantra] also. Therefore, the descriptions of prior approximation in all four tantra sets teach the stages of progress to higher and higher paths.

With regard to this, you need to differentiate well the steps for generating in [your mental] continuum mainly deity yoga and emptiness yoga. [Some,] without understanding such, hold that training in reciting a ritual formulation of a Means of Achievement[c] and the repetition of mantra during the rite are the meaning of approximation; they view the purpose of approximation as merely for the sake of engaging in the ritual formulations of initiation, consecration, and so forth. Those who seek understanding [of tantra within such misguided notions] are not seen to have gotten to the essentials of the path of any tantra set.

The descriptions—in the three tantra sets [Action, Performance, and Yoga] and by the great scholars who commented on their thought—of the calm abiding and special insight that are meditations on emptiness are seen to be similar to those in the master Kamalashīla's three works on the *Stages of Meditation,*[137] Ratnākarashānti's *Quintessential Instructions on the Perfection of Wisdom,*[138] Asaṅga's Treatises on the Grounds, Maitreya's Doctrines, and so forth. I have explained at length and in detail in my *Stages of the Path Common to the Vehicles:*[139]

- the reasons for the order of cultivating special insight after calm abiding
- how until gaining the two pliancies [mental and physical] you have a similitude of special insight and how after gaining them you have a fully qualified special insight

---

a *sngon du bsnyen pa.*

b *thob bya la khad nye bar byed pa.*

c *sgrub thabs, sādhana.*

- how both calm abiding and special insight are involved in meditating on selflessness
- the point at which union is achieved

and so forth. Hence, I will not elaborate on these here.

About the causes [created] during approximation for achieving feats, Buddhaguhya's *Introduction to the Meaning of the Tantra* says:[140]

> Even for [those making effort at][a] seals, secret-mantra, knowledge-mantra, and so forth, the rites of external offerings do indeed serve as causal branches of [achieving] feats, but due to the nature of things, feats are quickly bestowed just upon those who make effort mainly at repeating the essence-mantra and meditating [on a deity]. Therefore, those making effort for [feats] should make particular effort at these.

He speaks of the importance of deity meditation and performing repetition in complete fashion. Still, since he praises meditation on emptiness for purifying the obstructions preventing achievement of feats, it also is important. The same text says:[141]

> Through meditating on your deities—the perfect Buddhas and so forth—by way of mindfulness of them as [ultimately] aspectless and similarly through not having apprehension of yourself and all phenomena [as inherently existent], karmas and afflictive emotions preventing feats become non-existent. Then, whatever feat is desired is attained.

Also, concerning occasions of acting fiercely toward [that is, putting pressure on] the deity when feats are not achieved he says:[142]

> When yogis, even though they have pleased well the Secret Mantra Being, do not attain a feat as wished, they should especially observe

---

[a] This bracketed addition is taken directly from Buddhaguhya's *Introduction to the Meaning of the Tantra* (69.3.7), which reads *la brtson pa rnams* instead of *la sogs pa rnams:*

> *phyag rgya dang gsang sngags dang rig sngags* ***la brtson pa rnams*** *la yang phyi'i mchod pa'i cho ga rnams dngos grub kyi yan lag tu 'gyur mod kyi/*

la brtson pa rnams appears to be a better reading, since it parallels the other instances of *brtson* in the passage. Following Ḏzong-ka-ḇa's reading, the translation would read:

> Also, with respect to seals, secret-mantra, knowledge-mantra, and so forth the rites of external offerings do indeed serve as causal branches of [achieving] feats...

> the Truth Body of their own deity before and after the yoga of meditation on the great seal and so forth as well as before and after the yoga of repetition.

Therefore, if you meditate on emptiness before generating the great seal of divine body as well as after meditation and repetition, feats are speedily [achieved].

6. Feats

HOW TO ACHIEVE FEATS ONCE THE APPROXIMATION IS SERVICEABLE[a]

This section has three parts: how to achieve feats through concentration, how to achieve feats through repetition, and how to achieve feats through burnt offering.

How to Achieve Feats through Concentration

Having attained mastery over the general approximation and in particular the meditative stabilization of a subtle vajra as explained above, you should achieve the mundane and supramundane feats achieved through concentration.[143] There are two [varieties]:

- Through the descent of the wisdom[-being] upon having entered the maṇḍala [during initiation], mundane feats such as revealing where treasure is are achieved just through endeavor at them.
- The other type are those achieved through meditating until the arising of signs, to be explained below.

About this, the master Buddhaguhya asserts that the four seals [of exalted body, mind, speech, and activities] are achieved in the context of the wisdom-being's having entered yourself, but except for that, he asserts that all mundane and supramundane feats are achieved through offering and so forth to a wisdom-being set in front of yourself who does not enter you, while you dwell in the pride of merely a pledge-being. He states and refutes a system of other masters in which feats are achieved after causing the wisdom-being to enter yourself imagined as a pledge-being. The masters agree in asserting that all achievements of feats must be preceded by your own deity yoga.

---

[a] Perhaps Ḏzong-ka-ḇa does not call this section "fruit" (*'bras bu*) because, as Bu-ḏön's *Condensed General Presentation of the Tantra Sets* (Collected Works, vol. 14, 885.2-885.3) says, common feats—which include the "supreme" feat mentioned in this chapter that is a transformation of one's body into a semblance of a Buddha's physical form but is not an actual Buddha body—are merely methods **toward** achieving the final fruit.

Revealing Treasure[a]

If for the sake of achieving a special religious purpose—such as alleviating the poverty of yourself and others, and so forth—you [want to] achieve the feat of revealing treasure, you should do as the first section of the *Compendium of Principles* says:[b]

> Meditate on the form of a vajra
> In a treasure [pot] at your heart.
> If meditated,[c] you will see
> Treasure dwelling in the earth.

Contemplate a moon in a treasure-pot at your heart and on it a five-pointed vajra [the color of which accords with your lineage].[144] Repeat *vajranidhi*[d] and meditate until the signs arise. The signs are taken as [having a strong sense of] being able to see and feel [the vajra in the treasure-pot at the heart]. After performing repetition and meditation for the whole night upon the arising of those signs, go to the place where you hope there is treasure, make offerings and so forth to the deities, give food-offerings to the spirits, and bind and protect the treasure and place with the mantra and seal of Vajrasphoṭa.[e] Then, when meditation and repetition have been done, the treasure will be seen, whereupon you should dig up the earth and take it out.

Similarly, [the *Compendium of Principles Tantra*][145] also says that through having performed meditation and repetition [of *vajranidhi*],

---

[a] The sub-headings have been added for the sake of clarity.

[b] Stanza 236; Horiuchi, *Tattva-Saṃgrahaṃ,* 131: *vajrabimbaṃ nidhisthaṃ tu hṛdaye paribhāvayet / bhāvayan bhūmisaṃsthāni nidhānāni sa paśyati //;* D479, vol. *nya,* 28b.6. See Bu-d̄ön's *Practice of (Ānandagarbha's) "Rite of the Vajra Element [Great] Maṇḍala: Source of All Vajras": Wish-Fulfilling Gem,* vol. 12, 313.7. Bu-d̄ön uses a different translation that reads *dbyibs* instead of *gzugs.* The passage is cited by Buddhaguhya (P3324, vol. 70, 53.1.6), the translation being the same as that used by D̄zong-ka-b̄a.

[c] The tantra (D479, vol. *nya,* 28b.6) reads *bsgoms* ***nas,*** whereas D̄zong-ka-b̄a's text (172.7) reads *bsgoms* ***na.***

[d] Buddhaguhya (P3324, vol. 70, 53.3.3) says to use the mantra appropriate to your lineage. Bu-d̄ön's *Practice of (Ānandagarbha's) "Rite of the Vajra Element [Great] Maṇḍala: Source of All Vajras": Wish-Fulfilling Gem* (Collected Works, vol. 12, 314.1) lists the others as *ratnanidhi, padmanidhi,* and *karmanidhi.*

[e] *rdo rje lcags sgrog;* he is the guardian of the western door of the Vajra Element Great Maṇḍala.

meditating on a vajra in space or[a] meditating on yourself as a variegated [that is, crossed] vajra, you will come to know the presence of treasure in the place where [either of] those two vajras fall. Or,[146] through having done repetition of [*vajranidhī*][b] and meditation within meditating on a vajra on your tongue you will speak truthfully, "It is here."

Not Sinking into Water

If you [want to] achieve the feat of not sinking into water,[147] on the bank of a spring, and so forth, or in any place you wish, fill a great clay vessel with water, put it where it can be seen, and mentally say *vajrajvāla*.[c] Until the signs of tangibility and perceptibility arise, meditate in four sessions [daily] on the form of the water as having changed into solely the form of vajras, fused with each other such that the water turns into just the form of vajras. Then, make it such that, having become hard like a vajra, it can be touched by foot and hand. Draw a maṇḍala of the appropriate lineage there; perform the preliminary rites, and remain in that meditative stabilization for the entire night. Then, when you want to go onto the water, manifest this meditative stabilization, and just through this meditative equipoise go about, wander, and so forth on top of the water.

Going in Space

Meditate on the particles of space as variegated [that is, crossed] vajras,[d] which then fuse into vajra stairs, and familiarize and so forth as before, until they can be touched with foot and hand. Through this you can go to the peak of Mount Meru, and so forth.[148]

---

[a] That these are two separate practices is clear from Buddhaguhya's description of ways to accomplish this feat, these being the second and the fourth.

[b] Buddhaguhya's *Introduction to the Meaning of the Tantra* (P3324, vol. 70, 53.2.8) gives the example of *dharmanidhi*, not *padmanidhi*, as Bu-d̄ön (see 111, fnt. d) would suggest. The *Compendium of Principles Tantra* (D479, vol. *nya*, 29a.1) gives: *vajranidhī, ratnanidhī, dharmmanidhī, karmmanidhī*.

[c] As before, the mantra would be adjusted in accordance with your lineage.

[d] Buddhaguhya (P3324, vol. 70, 54.2.8) uses the older term "crossed vajra" (*rdo rje rgya gram*), for which Ḏzong-ka-ḇa (173.7) substitutes "variegated vajra" (*sna tshogs rdo rje*); the two terms have the same meaning.

Knowledge-Mantra Bearer[149]

With regard to achieving the feat of a Knowledge-Mantra Bearer[a] perform the rites of offering in extensive form, and having meditated on a subtle vajra, repeat any of the four essence-mantras, *vajradhara* and so forth [that is, *ratnadhara*, *padmadhara*, and *karmadhara*].[150] Contemplating [yourself in][151] the full form of the Knowledge-Mantra Bearer, concordant with the lineage of the individual section, as dwelling on a moon, meditate until the signs of tangibility and perceptibility arise. Then, if, having made offering to the deity [in whom you place] faith, you remain through the entire night within this meditative stabilization, the exalted wisdom-being who is your deity will come and bestow the feat of a Knowledge-Mantra Bearer as meditated. [The *Compendium of Principles*] describes the achievement of many such common feats.

Physical Transformation

If you wish to achieve the supreme feat,[b] generate yourself into the body of any of the five Ones-Gone-Thus, say *vajradhātu*, and contemplate all quarters of the sky as filled with tiny Buddha bodies.[152] Then, when the wind [breath] moves outside [that is, when exhaling], imagine that all those bodies are brightened, and when gathering the wind [that is, inhaling], hold them at your heart like fresh butter melting into sand. Through making effort at meditating nothing other than this and taming the assumption of bad states of the three doors [body, speech, and mind], meditate until you and others see [deities filling the sky].[153] When the signs arise, do as explained before—drawing a maṇḍala and so forth—whereby you will turn into a Bodhisattva Knowledge Bearer who holds the form of a perfect Buddha [that is, not an actual Buddha body, but a similitude of one].

Also, for the One-Gone-Thus lineage,[c] you should assume the pride of

---

[a] *rig sngags 'chang gi dngos grub;* it is called *rig 'dzin gyi dngos grub* in Bu-d̄ön's *Practice of (Ānandagarbha's) "Rite of the Vajra Element [Great] Maṇḍala: Source of All Vajras": Wish-Fulfilling Gem,* in Collected Works, vol. 12, 314.2. For this feat, see the *Compendium of Principles Tantra* (D479, vol. *nya,* 29a.4).

[b] *Compendium of Principles Tantra,* Toh. 479, vol. *nya,* 29a.7. This is not the supreme feat of Buddhahood but the supreme among mundane, or common, feats.

[c] D̄zong-ka-b̄a paraphrases Buddhaguhya's *Introduction to the Meaning of the Tantra,* vol. 70, 57.3.3. Buddhaguhya does not identify these two feats specifically as supreme (*mchog*), whereas he identifies the feat of a Knowledge-Mantra Bearer as supreme (54.2.3).

the undifferentiability of yourself and the form of your deity—Vajrasattva and so forth—and, abandoning harm to the three doors [body, speech and, mind] every day, meditate. When breath is let out, fill all quarters of the sky with the form of your deity. In particular, contemplate everything that comes as objects of the senses and of memory in the form of your deity. Also, when contemplating them [in the form of the deity] consider them this way:

> All these have arisen from my conceptions. They are not perceived to be separate in the way that they are imagined. When analyzed with reasoning and scripture, they do not ultimately exist.[a]

Then, withdrawing again your mind together with the wind [that is, breath], observe your [own body as the] deity. When, at the end of familiarizing in this way, the signs are gained as explained earlier, draw a maṇḍala, make offerings, and perform meditation and repetition, staying the entire night. When that is done, your deity will come and will bestow [the supreme feat][b] upon the form already established of the great seal of exalted body of your deity.

For both of those [supreme feats], meditation within stopping vitality and exertion [that is, breath and distraction] is prescribed. With respect to both, even if due to weak meditation the feat, as explained, is not attained, [Buddhaguhya][154] says that feats of clairvoyance, [lengthening] the life span, [increasing] strength, physical enhancement, and so forth are achieved even without assiduous endeavor.

This feat [of physical transformation], achieved in such a way, appears to be the best feat to be achieved initially by the supreme trainees of Yoga Tantra. In Action and Performance Tantra the achievement of the feat of a

---

a Buddhaguhya's reading (P3324, vol. 70, 57.3.8-57.4.1) is seemingly different:

> All these have arisen from my conceptions. Indeed, **just as they are conceptualized, so do they appear individually**, but since this contradicts reasoning and scripture, their nature does not at all ultimately exist.

> *'di rnams thams cad ni bdag gi rnam par rtog pa las byung ba ste/ ji ltar rnam par brtags pa de bzhin du so sor snang bar 'gyur mod kyi/ rigs pa dang lung dang 'gal bas 'di rnams kyi ngo bo nyid ni gang yang don dam par yod pa ma yin no/*

b This is the great seal of exalted body itself according to Ḍzong-ka-ḅa, even though it might seem to indicate Buddhahood. Ḍzong-ka-ḅa's statement, two paragraphs later, that it is the "best feat to be achieved **initially** by the supreme trainees of Yoga Tantra" makes his position clear.

Knowledge Bearer explained earlier appears to be a great feat of body [whereas here it is a lesser variety].[155]

How to Achieve Feats through Repetition

Those who achieve feats by way of repetition, having meditated on themselves as a deity, complete the prior approximation[a] by repeating the essence-mantra of the One-Gone-Thus lineage one hundred and eight times in each of four sessions each day over four months.[156]

Physical Transformation[157]

Then, if you wish to achieve the supreme feat, having first performed the yoga of your deity in the presence of a painting of that deity, perform repetition—as explained before—in each of four [daily] sessions over four months.[b] Then, at dawn the feat of the form of your deity is attained.

Pledge Seal

If you wish to achieve the feat of the pledge seal,[158] first do the approximation as explained before [see 110]. Then, in front of the form of your deity in a painting, in each of four sessions construct the pledge seal of Sattvavajrī of the One-Gone-Thus lineage, and without loosening that [hand-configuration], perform repetition. In general,[c] repeat the mantra until a hundred thousand have passed. Then, having constructed this seal, perform repetition the entire night. If you become tired during this period, loosen the seal, relieve tiredness, and constructing the seal again, repeat [the mantra].

If, having made your mind single-pointed in this way, you see the pledge seal flaming when constructed on top of your head,[159] you can fly

---

[a] Earlier, "prior approximation" referred to the yogas with and without signs, which comprise the first phase within the division of practices into approximation, achieving feats, and activities (*bsnyen, sgrub, las*). Here, it is the procedure described at the end of chapter three (see 89ff.) for those unable to do deity yoga in four sessions. Since the source is the Continuation of the Continuation of the *Compendium of Principles Tantra* (D479, vol. *nya,* 64.5.8), this mode of achieving feats is not for those who can do deity yoga, as is confirmed by the prescription to do repetition in the presence of a painting of the deity.

[b] This appears to be a second set of four months.

[c] Exceptions could occur when achievement of the feat happens before the complete count has passed, or when, due to non-achievement, an even greater count is required.

upon constructing the seal. When [wanting to] fly thus, through constructing the seal and just raising it up[160] you will be able to fly unimpededly in the sky.

If, from having constructed this pledge seal at the point between your eyes[161] and having performed repetition, you see it moving, then merely through constructing the seal you will be able to show yourself to others in whatever form you wish. If from holding the seal at your heart[162] and performing repetition you fly, you will attain the feat of invisibility merely through constructing the seal.

If the seal issues forth sounds, through constructing all or any of the individual seals of all the deities of the One-Gone-Thus lineage and repeating your essence-mantra you will be able to perform the activities as described in their individual texts.

Protection[163]

Furthermore, having first done approximation for four months and then performed repetition in the presence of your deity in four sessions for one month and then over an entire night, implant with the mantra of the individual [lineage] or the mantra of your deity a substance such as armor, a stick, a thread, mustard seed ashes, mustard seed, a vajra, a ritual dagger, an arrow, a bow, a sword, or mouse dung. When you hang this on [another's] body or give it in the hand, it can protect men, women, and children from demonic possession, fears of harm from humans, non-humans, and types of demons, as well as protect them from harmers, freeing them from all harm and fright. When there is apprehension about the arising of fright from enemies, opponents, fire, and water or the harm of contagion and sickness in a town, city, district, and so forth, if you create protection as [described just] above, [the area] will be freed from those frights.

Diagnosing Possession through Descent[164]

Furthermore, if—wishing to know about virtue and non-virtue [in the sense of determining from a spirit what should be done]—you want to cause it [to descend into a person or object], mix either white or red sandalwood in pure water and make it into a paste and repeat the mantra once into it. If [the person or object] is touched by it or by the constructed seal of a vajra,[a]

---

[a] For this hand-configuration and the next, see seals 7 and 8.

an iron hook, and so forth, or a cast image, and so forth, and [the spirit] descends, then once it has descended, [the person or object] will utter what [the situation is and what should be done, whereby you] will [be able to] pacify demons, and so forth.

Finding Lost Articles through Descent[165]

If, having done the same as above to a pot made of copper, clay, wood, and so forth, [you seek a spirit's] descent, it will descend, and [the person or object] will be able to indicate where to go to a lost article or[a] will be able to show who has taken it.

Physical Displays through Descent[166]

Similarly, during the final stage of performing the three stages[b] as described above, put a vajra made from wood inside peacock tails laid together, and tie it on the crown of your head. Pressing it with the pledge seal of Sattvavajrī, perform repetition until all seals[c] have entered. Once the signs[d] arise, through turning those feathers in a circle you will be able to display all forms, to display all activities for the welfare of the world, to display the Conquerors of the ten directions as well as their retinues, and also to display yourself in the body of a Buddha.

Controlling Another's Mind[167]

First do the approximation over four months; then, in the presence of your deity construct the above-mentioned pledge seal [of Sattvavajrī], and do one hundred and eight repetitions in four periods [each day] for one month. When that is finished, draw a maṇḍala, and then, constructing the pledge seal, perform repetition for an entire night, due to which the seal will be

---

[a] "Or" may indicate that what follows is a gloss of the former, since Buddhaguhya's *Introduction to the Meaning of the Tantra* (P3324, vol. 70, 65.3.4) does not have what follows. The meaning of "indicate" may be that the object or person entered goes there.

[b] The three stages are approximation for four months, approximation for a month in four sessions daily, and repetition all night.

[c] The meaning is unclear. According to Lati Rin-bo-chay, "all seals" here may refer to all the female beings called Seals.

[d] The "signs" may be the fact that all the Seals have entered. Again, the meaning is unclear.

seen as flaming. After that, enter into the mind of the sentient being whom you want to control, and fused with it, perform repetition, whereby that person will come under your control. [This and the preceding four practices] are the activities of protection, descent, and control.

Love and so forth

Buddhaguhya's *Introduction to the Meaning of the Tantra*[168] also describes how to achieve meditative stabilizations of love and so forth by performing repetition.

With respect to those, Buddhaguhya's *Introduction to the Meaning of the Tantra* and Padmavajra's commentary on it describe the four postures,[169] modes of recitation during repetition,[170] mental thoughts,[171] and modes of gazing[172]—as well as the individual pledges, accumulation of the collections [of merit and wisdom], the rosary for counting,[173] how to count [the repetition] with the hand,[174] and so forth. They collected these from the tantras, describing them in complete rites.

How to Achieve Feats through Burnt Offerings

Having first done the yoga of the deity for the individual hearth of pacifying ill-deeds, increasing lineage, and so forth, make burnt offering daily. It is explained that having done it until the signs—such as the pacification of ill-deeds in yourself or others—arise, the individual activity is achieved.

Thus, with regard to the three lower tantras [Action, Performance, and Yoga] it is necessary to know this mode through which you quickly progresses on the path: first maintaining the purity of the pledges and vows which are the source of feats, then gaining ability through striving at the yogas with and without signs in four sessions, and then achieving common and uncommon feats. It is not suitable to assert that you proceed on the path [of the three lower tantras merely] through a combination of wind, repetition, emptiness, and deity yogas [without the enhancement of achieving common feats]. Since the three lower tantras do not have the complete essentials of the stage of generation and do not have the essentials of the stage of completion, it is necessary to progress on the path through [also] achieving special feats.

So that the essentials of that [process] might be known I have expounded a little here based on Buddhaguhya's *Introduction to the Meaning of the Tantra* and its commentary written by the master Padmavajra.[a] They show—in accordance with the first section [of the *Compendium of Principles*]—the modes of achieving feats, scattered about in the tantra, which they collected together well.

The supreme ambrosia arisen from the churning
Of the ocean of milk, the glorious *Compendium of Principles,*
Supreme of all the Yoga Tantras,
By the churning sticks that are the texts by the three experts[b]

Is this [path system] in which, ripened by stainless initiation and abiding in the pledges,
One repeats [mantra] and meditates in four sessions,
Thereby training well the mind of the three yogas
Joining together the exalted body, speech, and mind

Of your special deity and your own three doors[c]
Whereby, upon engaging in any of the three approaches[d]
For achieving feats, the supreme is bestowed by your deity,
Due to which you easily traverse the good path [to Buddhahood].

Therefore, although knowing the stages of constructing seals
And the mere stages of ritual formulation
Is claimed [by some] to be knowledge of the meaning of Yoga Tantras,
They still need to seek the essentials of the path.

Thus ends the fourth section of *Revealing All Secret Topics, the Stages of the Path to a Great Vajradhara,* called "Stages of Progressing on the Path in Yoga Tantra."

---

a *skal bzang rdo rje;* the text is the *Commentarial Explanation of (Buddhaguhya's) "Introduction to the Meaning of the Tantra."*

b Buddhaguhya, Shākyamitra, and Ānandagarbha; see 18.

c Body, speech, and mind.

d Concentration, repetition, and burnt offering.

III: SUPPLEMENT

by Ke-drup-ge-lek-b̄el-sang

1. Five Manifest Enlightenments

from Ke-drup's
Extensive Explanation of the Format of the General Tantra Sets[175]

[The Yoga Tantra explanation of how the Teacher, the Supramundane Victor, became completely and perfectly buddhafied] is set forth in the two, the *Compendium of Principles,* which is the root tantra, and the *Vajrashekhara,* which is an explanatory tantra. The three—the masters Shākyamitra, Buddhaguhya, and Ānandagarbha[a]—who commented on the thought of those [tantras] were renowned in the country of Superiors [India] as the three humans expert in Yoga.

The System of Shākyamitra and Buddhaguhya

Our teacher the Supramundane Victor is asserted to be a fully qualified [that is to say, actual] tenth-ground Bodhisattva from the time he took birth as a son of King Shuddhodana through his practice of asceticism on the bank of the Nairañjanā River. When he had practiced asceticism there for six years, he entered into the meditative absorption called "the great of the great fourth concentration," also called "the highest limit of the four concentrations," "the immovable meditative stabilization," and "the meditative stabilization pervading space." At that time all the Buddhas of the ten directions gathered together and roused him from that meditative stabilization with the sound of snapping fingers. They said, "You cannot become completely and perfectly purified just through this meditative stabilization."

He asked, "Then how is it done?" Thereupon, they led him to the Highest Pure Land; leaving his fruition body on the bank of the Nairañjanā River, the mental body of the Bodhisattva Sarvārthasiddhi[b] went to the Highest Pure Land. After all the Buddhas of the ten directions conferred on him the raiment initiation,[c] that is to say, the crown initiation, they caused him to cultivate, in series, the five manifest enlightenments. At the end of completing the five manifest enlightenments, he was completely and perfectly buddhafied as the Complete Enjoyment Body, Mahāvairochana.

---

a The historical order is Buddhaguhya, Shākyamitra, and Ānandagarbha.

b *don thams cad grub pa;* this is what Siddhārtha is called in the *Compendium of Principles Tantra.*

c *gos kyi dbang.*

Having become buddhafied, he performed the four types of miracles [of magnificent blessing, conferring initiation, meditative stabilization, and exalted activity]. Proceeding to the peak of Mount Meru, he set forth the Yoga Tantras. Then, proceeding to the land of humans [India] he re-entered his fruition body on the bank of the Nairañjanā River. Rising, he engaged in displaying the manner of subjugating demons, becoming completely and perfectly buddhafied, and so forth.

The System of Ānandagarbha

At the end of accumulating the collections for three periods of countless eons, when [the Bodhisattva Sarvārthasiddhi] was a tenth-ground Bodhisattva in his last lifetime, in the Highest Pure Land he entered into meditative equipoise on the meditative stabilization pervading space. At that time, all the Buddhas of the ten directions gathered and roused him from that meditative stabilization through the sound of snapping their fingers. They said, "You cannot become completely and perfectly purified just through this meditative stabilization."

He asked, "Then how is it done?" Thereupon, all the Buddhas of the ten directions conferred the crown initiation, after which they caused him to cultivate, in series, the five manifest enlightenments. At the end of completing those, he became buddhafied as the Complete Enjoyment Body, Mahāvairochana. Having become buddhafied, he performed the four types of miracles. Proceeding to the peak of Mount Meru, he set forth the Yoga Tantras. Then he displayed the manner of the twelve deeds, taking birth in the land of humans as the son of King Shuddhodana.

The Five Manifest Enlightenments

There are five manifest enlightenments in terms of the miraculous history of the Teacher and five manifest enlightenments in terms of the practice of trainees who are his followers.

1. About those, after all the Buddhas of the ten directions conferred the crown initiation on the Bodhisattva Sarvārthasiddhi, they caused him to meditate on the meaning of the mantra *citta-prativedhaṃ karomi* ("I experience the mind.") Furthermore, through meditating by means of that, in meditative equipoise he directly realized his own mind's noumenon, the sixteen emptinesses, pure nature, and in subsequent attainment, having risen from that, he directly saw his own mind's noumenal pure nature in the aspect of a moon disc at his own heart. Through that, he gained the mirror-like exalted wisdom, the entity of Akṣhobhya. The name of this manifest

enlightenment is "manifest enlightenment from individual investigation."

When this is applied to the stages of practice by subsequent trainees, uttering "*citta-prativedhaṃ karomi,*" meditate on your own mind's noumenal pure nature, sixteen emptinesses symbolized by the sixteen vowels, which thoroughly transforms into the aspect of a moon disc at your heart [marked by the sixteen vowels].

2. After that, all the Buddhas of the ten directions caused the Bodhisattva Sarvārthasiddhi to meditate on the meaning of the mantra *oṃ bodhicittaṃ utpādayāmi* ("*Oṃ* I am causing the mind of enlightenment to be generated.") Furthermore, through meditating by means of that, in meditative equipoise he directly realized the noumenal emptiness of his mind as devoid of adventitious defilements, and in subsequent attainment he directly saw the noumenal emptiness of his mind devoid of adventitious defilements in the aspect of a [second] full moon disc at his heart. Through that, he gained the exalted wisdom of equality, the entity of Ratnasambhava. The name of this manifest enlightenment is "manifest enlightenment from generating the mind of supreme enlightenment."

When this is applied to the stages of practice by subsequent trainees, uttering "*oṃ bodhicittaṃ utpādayāmi,*" meditate on your mind's noumenal emptiness, devoid of adventitious defilements, symbolized by the consonants, which thoroughly transforms into the aspect of a [second] full moon disc at your heart [marked by the consonants].

3. After that, all the Buddhas caused him to meditate on the meaning of the mantra *tiṣṭha-vajra* ("stable vajra"). Through meditating [by means of that], he vividly saw just that previous all-good mind of enlightenment in the aspect of a white five-pointed vajra standing upright on the moon disc at his heart. Through that, he gained the exalted wisdom of individual analysis, the entity of Amitābha. The name of this manifest enlightenment is "enlightenment from the stable vajra."

When this is applied to the stages of practice by subsequent trainees, uttering "*tiṣṭha-vajra,*" meditate on a white five-pointed vajra at your heart.

Concerning this, I will speak about the meaning of "original vajra." "Original" means initial; also, with respect to the meaning of initial, when—in order for one who earlier had not become buddhafied to **newly** become fully purified—the five manifest enlightenments are meditated in stages, the white five-pointed vajra seen at their own heart is called an **original** vajra.

Question: What is the reason it is definitely a five-pointed vajra?

Answer: It is five-pointed in order to symbolize that each of the five manifest enlightenments, which are meditated in stages when you are becoming fully purified, actualizes one each of the five exalted wisdoms.

4. Then, all the Buddhas of the ten directions conferred the name initiation on the Bodhisattva Sarvārthasiddhi. Switching from the name "Sarvārthasiddhi," they designated him "Bodhisattva Vajradhātu." Then, they caused him to meditate on the meaning of the mantra *vajra-ātmako 'haṃ* ("Having a vajra nature am I.") Through meditating [by means of that], the vajra-elements of exalted body, the vajra-elements of exalted speech, and the vajra-elements of exalted mind of all Buddhas entirely and manifestly entered into the white five-pointed vajra at his heart, and he directly saw that vajra as established from the minute vajra particles of all the Ones-Gone-Thus. Through that, he gained the exalted wisdom of achieving activities, the entity of Amoghasiddhi. The name of this manifest enlightenment is "manifest enlightenment from the vajra essence."

When this is applied to the stages of practice by subsequent trainees, uttering "*vajra-ātmako 'haṃ,*" meditate on the white five-pointed vajra at your heart as emitting rays of light in the ten directions, through which the vajra-elements of exalted body, the vajra-elements of exalted speech, and the vajra-elements of exalted mind of all the Ones-Gone-Thus entirely enter into the white five-pointed vajra at your heart.

5. Then, all the Buddhas of the ten directions caused the Bodhisattva Vajradhātu to meditate on the meaning of the mantra *oṃ yathā sarvatathāgatās tathā 'haṃ* ("As all the Ones-Gone-Thus are, so am I.") Through meditating [by means of that], the vajra and moons at his heart were thoroughly transformed, manifesting as the Complete Enjoyment Body Mahāvairochana adorned with the thirty-two major marks and eighty beauties, being completely and perfectly buddhafied. Through that, he gained the exalted wisdom of the element of attributes, the entity of Vairochana. The name of this manifest enlightenment is "manifest enlightenment from the equality of all Ones-Gone-Thus."

When this is applied to the stages of practice by subsequent trainees, uttering "*oṃ yathā sarvatathāgatās tathā 'haṃ,*" the vajra as well as the moons at your heart thoroughly transform into the exalted body of Vairochana, on which you meditate.

Having become buddhafied, he performed the four types of miracles [of magnificent blessing, conferring initiation, meditative stabilization, and exalted activity]. While the Complete Enjoyment Body remained in the

Highest Pure Land, he emanated a four-faced Vairochana, which, proceeding to the peak of Mount Meru, performed deeds such as setting forth the fundamental Yoga Tantra, the *Compendium of Principles.* Having gone to the land of humans, he displayed the manner of subjugating demons, becoming completely and perfectly buddhafied, and so forth.[a]

[a] For the First Panchen Lama Lo-sang-chö-ḡyi-gyel-tsen's exposition of the five manifest enlightenments, see the Appendix, 154ff.

2. Four Seals

from Ke-drup's
Extensive Explanation of the Format of the General Tantra Sets[176]

The presentation of how to train in the stages of the path has five parts: etymology of seal, divisions, order, purpose and benefit of seal-impression, and how to do seal-impression.

Etymology of Seal

The meaning of seal-impression is that it is not suitable to pass beyond [what, for example, has been attested to]. Therefore, in the mode of deity meditation seal-impression with the four seals [indicates that it is] not suitable to pass beyond that mode [of imagination of yourself as a deity].

Divisions of Seals

There are four seals—great seal, pledge seal, doctrine seal, and action seal. There are also three seals:

- basal-seals that are the objects of purification
- path-seals that are the means of purification
- fruit-seals that are states of purification.

With respect to basal-seals that are the objects being purified, the four—ordinary body, mind, speech, and their activities—are respectively the main bases of purification of the four: great seal, pledge seal, doctrine seal, and action seal.

Also, the four—desire, hatred, bewilderment, and miserliness—are correlated as the bases of purification of the four, the great seal and so forth. The reason for this is that earlier the four lineages of trainees with predominant desire and so forth are correlated respectively as the trainees of the four sections [of the *Compendium of Principles Tantra*], and the four sections are correlated respectively with the four seals.

Furthermore, the four constituents of earth, water, fire, and wind are respectively correlated as the bases of purification. The reason for this is that the four seals are correlated with the lineages of the four sections, and within the four lineages:

- the purified earth constituent is Vairochana
- the purified water constituent is Akṣhobhya
- the purified fire constituent is Amitābha
- the purified wind constituent is Amoghasiddhi.

With respect to the path-seals that are the means of purification, the four sections [of the *Compendium of Principles Tantra*] are correlated with the four seals. This is due to the fact that the paths taught in the first section are mainly paths of the great seal of body; the paths taught in the second are mainly paths of the pledge seal of mind; the paths taught in the third are mainly paths of the doctrine seal of speech; and the paths taught in the fourth are mainly paths of the action seal of activities.

Moreover, the paths such as the three meditative stabilizations, which are taught at the point of the great maṇḍala in each section, are mainly paths of the great seal of body, and likewise the paths taught in the context of the [other] three maṇḍalas—retention, doctrine, and action maṇḍalas—are mainly paths respectively of the pledge seal of mind, the doctrine seal of speech, and the action seal of activities.[a] Therefore, those are correlated respectively [as the path-seals that are the means of purification].

Each deity, Vairochana and so forth, of each of the four maṇḍalas [set forth in each of the four sections of the tantra] are impressed with the four seals. Also, each of those seals is of two types—a seal that is the meaning symbolized and a seal that is the symbol. The seals that are the symbols also are divided into two types, seals that are external symbols and seals that are internal symbols. Thereby, [each of the four seals] has three types: [the meaning symbolized, external symbol, and internal symbol].

With respect to the great seal [of body]:

- The meaning symbolized is the physical aspect of that particular deity—Vairochana and so forth.

---

[a] Each of the four sections teaches the three meditative stabilizations of initial preparation, supreme royal maṇḍala, and supreme royal activities:

- the three meditative stabilizations set forth at the point of the basic maṇḍala in each section involve mainly the great seal of exalted body
- the three meditative stabilizations set forth at the point of the retention maṇḍala in each section involve mainly the pledge seal
- the three meditative stabilizations set forth at the point of the doctrine maṇḍala in each section involve mainly the doctrine seal
- and the three meditative stabilizations set forth at the point of the action maṇḍala in each section involve mainly the action seal.

- The external symbolizing seal is a configuration of the hands[a] constructed in accordance with an aspect residing in the nature of that exalted body.[b]
- The internal symbolizing seal is the simultaneous clear imagination of yourself as the body of the particular deity.

With respect to the pledge seal:

- The meaning symbolized is the exalted non-conceptual wisdom—the exalted mind—of that particular deity, considered as appearing in the aspect of a hand-symbol[c] [that is, an article such as a vajra held in the hand].
- The external symbolizing seal is a configuration of the hands constructed in accordance with an aspect of that.[177]
- The internal symbolizing seal is the simultaneous contemplation of the exalted non-conceptual wisdom—of the particular deity as whom you are meditating—as appearing in the aspect of a hand-symbol.

With respect to the doctrine seal:

- The meaning symbolized is the sixty branches of euphonic speech teaching the eighty-four thousand bundles of doctrine of that particular deity.
- The external symbolizing seal is letters set in such places as the tongue, throat, and so forth of the deity as whom you are meditating.
- The internal symbolizing seal is the contemplation of the speech—of the particular deity as whom you are visualizing yourself—as appearing in the aspect of written letters.

[With respect to the action seal:[178]

- The meaning symbolized is that particular deity's exalted activities effecting the welfare of sentient beings.
- The external symbolizing seal is a hand-configuration constructed in accordance with an aspect of those activities.

---

a *lag pa'i 'du byed.*

b As examples of the four seals, see those of Vajrasattva (seals 1-4). The doctrine seal of Vajrasattva that is depicted there is for those mainly performing yoga without signs, which is the hand-configuration of meditative equipoise. The doctrine seal of Vajrasattva for those mainly performing yoga with signs is the same as the great seal of Vajrasattva.

c *phyag mtshan.*

- The internal symbolizing seal is the contemplation of your own body clearly appearing as the exalted body—of the particular deity as whom you are visualizing yourself—effecting the welfare of sentient beings.]

With regard to the seals that are the fruit of purification, these are the four—exalted body, mind, speech, and activities of the effect state [as a Buddha]—correlated respectively with the four, the great seal, and so forth. These are also the four exalted wisdoms correlated respectively with the four seals. The reason for this is that the four exalted wisdoms are correlated with the four sections, and the four sections are correlated with the four seals. Furthermore, the four exalted bodies are correlated respectively with the four seals due to the fact that the four exalted bodies are associated with the four sections, and the four sections are correlated with the four seals.

ORDER OF THE FOUR SEALS

Seal-impression with the four seals is done after you have generated yourself as the pledge-being and caused the wisdom-being to enter into the pledge-being. Seal-impression with the four seals is not done to either the pledge-being alone or the wisdom-being alone because the purpose of seal-impression with the four seals is to make the four—the exalted body, speech, mind, and activities of the wisdom-being—inseparable from those four of the pledge-being after they have been mixed [through having caused the wisdom-being to enter into the pledge-being], and either of those alone does not have anything to be mixed. This is the same for both self-generation and generation [of a deity] in front. That this is so [is indicated] in the *Shrīparamādya Tantra:*

> That which is impressed with whatsoever seal
> Has the nature of that [seal].

Also the *Vajrashekhara* says:[179]

> The partial of either the uppermost of all
> Or the lower is to be abandoned.

"The uppermost of all" is the wisdom-being and the "lower" is the pledge-being. It is saying that you should abandon seal-impression of the partial, that is to say, the limited [merely the wisdom-being or merely the pledge-being].

Concerning this, in the system of the master Ānandagarbha it is asserted that they are performed in the order of the pledge seal [of exalted mind], the doctrine seal [of exalted speech], the action seal [of exalted activities], and the great seal [of exalted body]. In the system of the two masters, Buddhaguhya and Shākyamitra, it is asserted that they are performed in the order of the great seal, pledge seal, action seal, and doctrine seal. Previous [scholars] expressed the assertion of those two masters in a way that appears to be a case of not having understood their assertion. Some say:

Those two masters' assertion is not correct:

- because Ānandagarbha's commentary on the first part of the *Compendium of Principles Tantra* says that through the pledge seal [the non-duality of yourself and the deity is newly] achieved; through the doctrine seal you are set [in powerful speech]; through the action seal you apply yourself to activities; and through the great seal you are set in meditative equipoise in the manner of thoroughly dwelling [on the fact of the non-duality of yourself and the deity that has already been achieved],[180] and
- because each deity must be generated by way of sixteen doors:

  [1-4] the four seals
  [5-8] the four: summoning, causing to enter, binding, and controlling
  [9-10] the two, bestowing initiation and blessing into magnificence
  [11-12] the two, meditative stabilization and offering
  [13-14] the two, seal[-mantra] and essence[-mantra]
  [15-16] the two, mantra and knowledge[-mantra]

  but in the system of these two masters the sixteen doors are not complete.

[That is what those earlier scholars say about Buddhaguhya's and Shākyamitra's system, but those earlier scholars] are wrong because it does not appear that Ānandagarbha explained that the reason why the order is limited to this way is that the meaning of "Through the pledge seal [the non-duality of yourself and the deity is newly] achieved" and so forth is such-and-such. Hence, it appears that [the above criticism] comes to be that "The system of those two masters is not correct because of disagreeing with Ānandagarbha." Consequently, what could [those earlier scholars] say to the proposition that

"The system of Ānandagarbha is also incorrect because of disagreeing with Buddhaguhya"? Also, [those earlier scholars] need to set out the reasons why when [these topics] are treated according to the system of those two masters [Buddhaguhya and Shākyamitra], the sixteen doors [in Ānandagarbha's way] are incomplete.

Question: Then in your system what is the assertion of these two masters [Buddhaguhya and Shākyamitra]?

Answer: In accordance with the meaning of the statement in Chandrakīrti's *Supplement to (Nāgārjuna's) "Treatise on the Middle,"*[181] "Since [conceptual] minds [and mental factors] have ceased, it [the Truth Body] is actualized by the [Complete Enjoyment] Body," the Truth Body must be actualized on the basis of the Complete Enjoyment Body, and therefore seal-impression with the great seal of exalted body is done first. Since, without actualizing the Truth Body, activities spontaneous and without striving do not arise, the pledge seal is done second. Since activities, spontaneous and without striving, arise upon having actualized the Truth Body, the action seal is done after the pledge seal. Since teaching doctrine itself with the sixty branches of euphonic speech is the main of activities, impression with the doctrine seal is done after the action seal.

Question: Also then, in your system what is the assertion of the master Ānandagarbha?

Answer: Through the pledge seal [of exalted mind] you newly achieve a previously unachieved non-duality of yourself and the deity, whereupon you are set in meditative equipoise on the meaning of suchness [emptiness]; hence, the pledge seal is done first. Since without being set in single-pointed meditative equipoise on the meaning of suchness and without speech having become of powerful capacity, you cannot incite a supramundane deity to activity, the doctrine seal [of exalted speech] is done second. Since you engage in exalted activity upon the mind's being set in meditative equipoise on suchness and upon speech having become of powerful capacity, the action seal [of exalted activity] is done third. [Since] it is the case that after the great seal you are to be set in meditative equipoise in the manner of thoroughly dwelling on the meaning of the already accomplished non-duality of yourself and the deity, without first establishing this non-duality there is no way you can set in meditative equipoise on the meaning of this non-duality; hence, seal-impression with the great seal [of exalted body] is indicated [by Ānandagarbha] as being done afterward.

Question: Then, which of those two is taken as your own system?

Answer: It is permissible to do either of them. However, if you do [seal-impression] in dependence upon Ānandagarbha's *Rite of the Vajra Element Great Maṇḍala: Source of All Vajras,*[182] you must use just the system of Ānandagarbha.

PURPOSE AND BENEFIT OF SEAL-IMPRESSION

The main purpose is to transform the four—ordinary body, speech, and mind as well as activities—into the four, the exalted body, speech, mind, and activities of a Conqueror.

HOW TO DO SEAL-IMPRESSION

About this, there are four topics—cause giving rise to seals, rite of constructing the entities of the seals themselves, cause of achievement, and cause of mastery over what has been achieved.[a]

PLEDGE SEAL

Cause Giving Rise to a Pledge Seal

With respect to the cause giving rise to [pledge] seals, the tantra explains that all pledge seals arise from the vajra-binding. About this, someone [mistakenly] says:

> The two, Buddhaguhya's *Introduction to the Meaning of the Tantra* and Shākyamitra's *Ornament of Kosala,* explain that the vajra-binding is the cause of all seals, and this is in consideration of an indirect cause. The master Ānandagarbha explains that [such a cause] is not necessarily a cause, but he says this in consideration that it is not a direct cause [not that it is not a cause in general. Thus, all three scholars agree that the vajra-binding is an indirect cause of **all** seals, not just of all pledge seals.] First construct the vajra-binding, and then, from this, construct the pledge seal of Vairochana. Without loosening the vajra-binding that was initially constructed, the pledge seal of Vairochana [is constructed], from which the pledge seals of the other deities are constructed. Also, from

[a] Ke-drup does not treat the four as formal headings, but to make the translation more accessible I have treated them this way.

those the other [seals] are to be constructed in order.

This is incorrect because both the tantra and Ānandagarbha's *Rite of the Vajra Element Great Maṇḍala: Source of All Vajras* say, "All **pledge** seals arise from the vajra-binding," and say that "having constructed the vajra-binding" is to be affixed at the head of [instructions for] all **pledge** seals.

Rite of Constructing the Entity of a Pledge Seal Itself

One [scholar mistakenly] says, "[Uttering] '*vajrasattva*,' construct the vajra-binding; through it the eyes are blessed into magnificence." This is incorrect because "*vajrasattva*" is not a mantra blessing the eyes into magnificence but is the mantra of constructing the vajra-binding. Ānandagarbha's *Rite of the Vajra Element Great Maṇḍala: Source of All Vajras* says that "*vajradṛṣṭi*"[a] ("vajra-sight") is the mantra blessing the eyes into magnificence. Therefore, if it were not necessary to construct a vajra-binding prior to each pledge seal, it would also not be necessary to utter the mantra "*vajrasattva*" for each [which is obviously not the case].

Hence, through [uttering] "*vajrasattva*" construct the vajra-binding, and through looking with the eyes of exalted wisdom—which are the eyes blessed through [uttering] "*vajradṛṣṭi*"—think that you manifestly see the wisdom-being Vairochana dwelling in front [of yourself]. Then, through "*oṃ vajradhātvīshvarī*" construct the pledge seal of Vairochana, and with the four [syllables] "*jaḥ hūṃ baṃ hoḥ*" [the wisdom-being Vairochana] is respectively summoned, caused to enter, bound, and controlled, whereby yourself and the wisdom-being are made non-dual. Then, through "*vajrasattva*" imagine a sun-disk[b] behind Vairochana. Through "*vajrasattva samayastvam ahaṃ*" create pride in being an entity in which you are non-dual with the wisdom-being.

Cause of Achieving a Pledge Seal

About what is done after those seal-impressions, one [scholar mistakenly] says:

---

[a] The spelling of the mantra is taken from Lessing and Wayman (240, fnt. 41), who have drawn it from Ānandagarbha's text that Ke-drup here references; in their version Ke-drup has *vajra dṛḍha tiṣṭa* (240.22), whereas the Guru Deva edition (578.2) reads *vajra dṛḍha tiṣṭha*.

[b] *rgyab yol;* a halo.

> After having done seal-impression of all the deities, an original five-pointed vajra is on a moon disc at the heart of all the deities.

[However,] for the sense of the meditation, merely that is not sufficient. [Therefore] immediately after doing seal-impression, the exalted mind of Vairochana—just the exalted non-conceptual wisdom—is to be meditated upon in the aspect of a five-pointed white vajra on a moon [at the heart]. With your mind single-pointedly observing this, repeat the three general mantras each and their respective three mantras each. Observing this for a long time is the cause of achieving the seal.

Cause of Mastery over What Has Been Achieved

Then, meditation breaking down through reasoning your own aggregates and so forth into emptiness is the cause of mastery.

DOCTRINE SEAL

Cause Giving Rise to a Doctrine Seal

The cause giving rise to the doctrine seal is the verbal activity of expression. With respect to the mode of seal-impression, in the throat of the specific deity imagine *hrīḥ,* which turns into an eight-petalled red lotus. The petal on the axis of the tongue becomes the tongue, and on top of it a white five-pointed vajra rests on the lip. Bless it into magnificence with "*oṃ vajra-jihva*" ("*oṃ* vajra-tongue") and set the letters of their own doctrine, such as "*vajra-jñāna*" ("vajra-wisdom") and so forth, circling the center of the vajra. Uttering the syllables of doctrine in speech is the mode of seal-impression.

Rite of Constructing the Entity of a Doctrine Seal Itself & Cause of Achieving a Doctrine Seal

In the practice system of both Bu-d̄ön Rin-b̄o-chay and the Mountain Virtuous Ones[a] [that is, Ge-luk-b̄as], this doctrine seal [of exalted speech] is treated as involving construction of the great seal, which is a seal of body.[b] Concerning this, someone says, "It is not explained anywhere that the doctrine seal [of exalted speech] involves a seal of body." That is extremely

---

a *ri bo dge ldan pa.*

b *lus kyi phyag rgya.*

incorrect because the *Shrīparamādya Tantra* says:[183]

> Through the yoga
> Of all-attraction toward that [deity]
> Who is standing up or sitting or staying still
> All feats will be attained.

In commentary on this, Ānandagarbha's *Extensive Commentary on the Shrīparamādya*[184] says:

> Through uttering just this, you should meditate on an image of the respective deity who is standing or sitting. "Through the yoga of all-attraction" [indicates] the naturally pure entity [of the deity]. Through doing such, what will be achieved? "All feats will be attained." That is to say, through the doctrine seal [of exalted speech] of the deities in all lineages, all feats will be achieved.

The simultaneous composite of the three:

- uttering syllables of doctrine in speech, which [is indicated by] "through uttering just that"
- constructing a seal that is a physical expression concordant with the aspect of standing or sitting or the like of "the respective deity," that is to say, the deity who is to be impressed with the seal
- and setting your mind in meditative equipoise on the meaning of suchness

is the cause giving rise to the [doctrine] seal [of exalted speech]. If the great seal [of exalted body] is not constructed, the causes of achieving [the doctrine seal] would be incomplete; consequently, refuting construction of the great seal here is very unsuitable.

Cause of Mastery over What Has Been Achieved

With respect to the cause of mastering the doctrine seal [of exalted speech] from within non-dual profundity and manifestation, which involves physical manifestation in the aspect of the appropriate deity and mental single-pointed observation of the meaning of realizing suchness, the tongue together with the vajra [imagined] on it is pressed to the palate, and then a tiny vajra the size of a grain of barley is emitted and meditated at the tip of the nose. Through meditating on it until the signs of touchability and perceptibility arise, very great feats are achieved in dependence upon the doctrine seal. This is the measure of controlling the doctrine seal [of exalted speech].

ACTION SEAL

Cause Giving Rise to an Action Seal

The cause giving rise to the action seal is the vajra-fist.

Rite of Constructing the Entity of an Action Seal Itself

With respect to the mode of seal-impression [that is, construction of the action seal], set the right vajra fist on top of the left vajra fist, and preceded by lotus encircling, construct the great seal [of exalted body] of the particular deity without the respective hand-symbol. Utter the respective mantra, and when releasing the seal, snap the fingers, and imagine performing exalted activities.

Cause of Achieving an Action Seal

The cause of achieving [the action seal of exalted activities] is: When constructing the seal, meditate on a variegated [that is, crossed] vajra at the heart of the individual deities, and imagine that it is an entity of the exalted wisdom of achieving activities.

Cause of Mastery over What Has Been Achieved

With respect to the cause of mastering [the action seal of exalted activities], using mindfulness and introspection, cultivate continuous imagination of:

- all physical modes of behavior as a god's worshipping a god with dance and so forth
- all verbal statements and expressions as a god worshipping a god through song and so forth
- and even all food, drink, and so forth as a god worshipping a god.

Imagine that whereas their entity is undifferentiable from the deity and emptiness, they appear in the aspect of forms, sounds, and so forth. When if, through meditating that way, familiarization becomes stable, divine activities are achieved with all modes of physical and verbal activity, you have mastered [that is, brought under your control, the action seal of exalted activities].

GREAT SEAL

Cause Giving Rise to a Great Seal

The cause giving rise to the great seal [of exalted body] is mainly the vajra fist.

Rite of Constructing the Entity of a Great Seal Itself

The mode of seal-impression [that is, construction of the great seal] is to construct the great seal, which abides in the nature [of the divine body in the sense of corresponding in aspect with it]. This is the seal of supreme enlightenment, and so forth.

Cause of Achieving a Great Seal

The cause of achieving [the great seal of exalted body] is to meditate on a five-pointed original vajra at the heart of the individual deities.

Cause of Mastery over What Has Been Achieved

The cause of mastering [the great seal of exalted body] is to keep cultivating the deity yoga of non-dual profundity and manifestation until attaining steadiness. In consideration that this is easy to understand, it is not explicitly described [in the texts].

Question: When, having made the seal-impression of Vairochana, you make the seal-impression of Akṣhobhya, do you do it within that very meditation of yourself in the aspect of Vairochana or upon transforming into the aspect of Akṣhobhya? If it is according to the first way, you would be doing seal-impression of Vairochana and not seal-impression of Akṣhobhya. If it is according to the second way, would Akṣhobhya who is in the east move here [to the center], due to which the eastern quadrant would be meditated as empty, or would you meditate on two Akṣhobhyas?

Answer: Without yourself stirring from the aspect of Vairochana, you construct the seal of the eastern Akṣhobhya himself, gaze at the wisdom-being of Akṣhobhya residing in front [of him], and meditate on [the wisdom-being's] being summoned, entering, being bound, and being brought under control in him. Nevertheless, through Akṣhobhya mixing undifferentiably with the wisdom-being, you and the wisdom-being also become undifferentiably mixed because you and Akṣhobhya are being meditated as of one continuum. Through that, you also should understand that the other root deities [are to receive seal-impression and to be meditated in this way].

IV: Practical Outline of the Steps of the Path

formulated by Jeffrey Hopkins

The Practice of Yoga Tantra

Once a practitioner has received initiation and maintained its accompanying vows and pledges, the basic yoga is twofold, yoga with signs and yoga without signs. In the yoga with signs a concentrated mind, called calm abiding, is achieved. In the yoga without signs a profoundly powerful mind penetrating the nature of phenomena, called special insight, is achieved. The practice of these two types of yoga is called prior approximation, since it is a phase of approximating, or coming close to, the state of the deity, prior to achieving mundane and supramundane yogic feats.

Yoga with signs is performed in four sessions every day and progresses from initially observing a larger object—a single deity or multiple deities—to observing a very small object in order to bring about concentrative power. Whether a practitioner meditates on only a single deity or multiple deities depends upon whether only a student's initiation has been received or whether a master's initiation has also been received, and depends on the present capacity of the practitioner.

Let us start with laying out the steps of a student's yoga of four sessions observing a single deity. To do this, let us draw from D̄zong-ka-b̄a's and the Dalai Lama's explanations to create a step-by-step outline of the practices.

YOGA WITH SIGNS

YOGA OBSERVING A SINGLE DEITY IN FOUR SESSIONS FOR THOSE WHO HAVE OBTAINED A STUDENT'S INITIATION

The choice of deity is often determined by dropping a petal from above onto a separate maṇḍala, divided into quadrants and a center, to determine the lineage. Then:

Having performed self-protection, bathing with water, and again self-protection and place-protection, request your deity to sit in front of you.

Pay obeisance from each of the four directions, disclose ill-deeds, admire the merit of all beings, entreat the deity to turn the wheel of doctrine, supplicate the deity not to pass into nirvāṇa, make offering, dedicate the virtue of these practices to the welfare of all beings, generate an altruistic intention to become enlightened, take refuge, assume the Bodhisattva vows, and so forth.

Make the hand gestures ranging from the vajra-palms through the descent of the wisdom-being.

Perform self-generation by way of the five rites, called the five manifest enlightenments—the principles of mind, sattva, meditative stabilization, vajra, and Vajradhara.[a]

1. Uttering "*citta-prativedhaṃ karomi*" ("I experience the mind."), meditate on the emptiness of your mind, which transforms into the aspect of a moon disc at your heart marked with the sixteen vowels. This is called the rite of the mind principle and "manifest enlightenment from individual investigation."
2. Uttering "*oṃ bodhicittaṃ utpādayāmi*" ("*Oṃ* I am causing the mind of enlightenment to be generated."), meditate on your mind's noumenal emptiness, devoid of adventitious defilements, which transforms into a second full moon disc—marked with the thirty-six consonants—above the former, at your heart. This is called the rite of the sattva principle and "manifest enlightenment from generating the mind of supreme enlightenment."
3. Uttering "*tiṣṭha-vajra*" ("stable vajra"), meditate on a white five-pointed vajra at your heart. This is called the rite of the meditative stabilization principle and "enlightenment from the stable vajra."
4. Uttering "*vajra-ātmako 'haṃ*" ("Having a vajra nature am I."), meditate on the white five-pointed vajra at your heart as emitting rays of light in the ten directions, through which the vajra-elements of exalted body, the vajra-elements of exalted speech, and the vajra-elements of exalted mind of all the Ones-Gone-Thus entirely enter into the white five-pointed vajra at your heart. This is called the rite of the vajra principle and "manifest enlightenment from the vajra essence."
5. Uttering "*oṃ yathā sarvatathāgatās tathā 'haṃ*" ("As all the Ones-Gone-Thus are, so am I."), the vajra and moons at your heart thoroughly transform into the exalted body of Vairochana; meditate on the full body of the deity. This is called the

[a] For a detailed description of the five manifest enlightenments see 123ff.

Eight Yoga Tantra Seals

Demonstrated by Ven. Jhado Tulku, abbot emeritus of Namgyel Tantric College

1 Great seal of Vajrasattva

2 Pledge seal of Vajrasattva

3 Doctrine seal of Vajrasattva for yoga without signs

4 Action seal of Vajrasattva

5 Vajra-binding

6 Vajra-palms

7 Vajra

8 Iron hook

great seal principle, or Vajradhara principle, and "manifest enlightenment from the equality of all Ones-Gone-Thus."

You are now sitting in space as a deity. Imagine a lion seat in the middle of an inestimable mansion on Mount Meru on a series of stacked up elements—earth, water, fire, and wind.

Onto this you—as Vajrasattva or the correspondingly appropriate deity—descend from space and sit. You thereby mimic the descent of a deity.

Having said "*vajradhātu*" and constructed the seal of supreme enlightenment, imagine yourself as Vairochana, for instance.

Saying "*vajrasattva,*" emanate a Vajrasattva from your heart, setting him also on a lion seat, like your own, contemplated in front of yourself, like deity generation in front.

Reciting Vajrasattva's essence-mantra and constructing his great seal, contemplate yourself as Vajrasattva.

From the letter *hūṃ* at your heart emanate Huṃkara, and saying the mantra and making the seal of opening doors, mentally open the four doors of the maṇḍala.

With the mantra and seal of assembling the vajra deities gather the Buddhas.

Meditating on them as Vajrasattvas, praise them with the hundred and eight names.

Saying *jaḥ hūṃ baṃ hoḥ,* with application of mental goodness cause all the Ones-Gone-Thus to enter your own body.

To your divine body, which limitless Ones-Gone-Thus have been caused to enter, perform seal-impression with the four seals—pledge, doctrine, action, and great seals.[a]

Pledge Seal

- Through uttering "*vajrasattva*" construct the vajra-binding, and through looking with the eyes of exalted wisdom—which are the eyes blessed through uttering "*vajradṛṣṭi*"—think that you manifestly see the wisdom-being Vairochana dwelling in front of yourself. Then, through "*oṃ vajradhātvīshvarī*" construct the pledge seal of Vairochana, and with the four syllables "*jaḥ hūṃ baṃ hoḥ*" the wisdom-being Vairochana is respectively summoned, caused to enter, bound, and controlled, whereby yourself and the wisdom-being are made non-dual.

---

a As examples of the four seals, see those of Vajrasattva (seals 1-4).

Then, through "*vajrasattva*" imagine a sun-disk behind Vairochana. Through "*vajrasattva samayastvam ahaṃ*" create pride in being non-dual with the wisdom-being.

- Immediately after doing seal-impression, meditate on the exalted mind of Vairochana—the exalted non-conceptual wisdom itself—in the aspect of a five-pointed white vajra on a moon at the heart. With your mind single-pointedly observing this, repeat the three general mantras each and their respective three mantras.
- Meditate within breaking down through reasoning your own aggregates and so forth into emptiness.

Doctrine Seal

- In the throat of the specific deity imagine *hrīḥ,* which turns into an eight-petalled red lotus. The petal on the axis of the tongue becomes the tongue, and on top of it a white five-pointed vajra rests on the lip. Bless it into magnificence with "*oṃ vajra-jīhva*" ("*oṃ* vajra-tongue") and set the letters of their own doctrine, such as "*vajra-jñāna*" ("vajra-wisdom") and so forth, circling the center of the vajra.
- Set your mind in meditative equipoise on the meaning of suchness.
- Press your tongue together with the vajra imagined on it to your palate, and then a tiny vajra the size of a grain of barley is emitted from the vajra. Meditate on it at the tip of your nose.

Action Seal

- Set your right vajra fist on top of your left vajra fist, and then after lotus circling, construct the great seal of exalted body of the particular deity, meditating on a crossed vajra at the heart of the individual deity, imagining that it is an entity of the exalted wisdom of achieving activities. Utter the respective mantra, and when releasing the seal, snap your fingers, and imagine performing exalted activities.
- Utilizing mindfulness and introspection, cultivate continuous imagination of all physical modes of behavior as a god's worshipping a god with dance and so forth; all verbal statements and expressions as a god worshipping a god through song and

so forth; and even all food, drink, and so forth as a god worshipping a god.

Great Seal

- Within meditating on a five-pointed original vajra at the heart of the deity, from the vajra fist construct the great seal—the seal of supreme enlightenment, and so forth.
- Keep cultivating the deity yoga of non-dual profundity and manifestation until attaining steadiness.

Bless yourself with the pledge seal of the lineage.

Confer initiation on yourself with whatever the initiation of the lineage is.

Make offering to yourself with the four secret offerings by the Goddess of Charm and so forth.

Meditate on the great seal of exalted body, your own divine body.

Meditate on the three equalities, viewing (1) yourself, (2) all sentient beings, and (3) all the deities of the maṇḍala as equally without self, or inherent existence. View all phenomena as of one taste in the sphere of the absence of inherent existence.

Repeat the mantra of the specific deity. (Except for the single yoga of the one deity, for a practitioner doing only the student's yoga there is no great yoga in which all deities of the maṇḍala are meditated.)

In four sessions—in the morning, noon, afternoon and evening, and midnight[a]—for a year, or whatever time it takes, stop the mind from being distracted to anything other than the stages of the rite, and without letting the stages of meditation pass as mere verbiage, invoke images at each point.

Meditate until clear appearance like that of direct perception arises. That is taken as the measure of having initially generated the yoga in the continuum.

---

[a] According to Lati Rin-b̄o-chay, it is generally said that one should avoid having meditative sessions at dawn, noon, sunset, and midnight; thus, these four may refer to general periods of time.

YOGA OBSERVING A COMPLETE MANDALA OF DEITIES IN FOUR SESSIONS FOR THOSE WHO HAVE OBTAINED A MASTER'S INITIATION

If you have obtained a master's initiation and wish to bestow initiation on a student, you must:

1. Perform the great yoga of self-completion,[a] which means to meditate on the full number of deities in the respective maṇḍala by doing either:
   - an extensive divine approximation cultivating, without any abbreviation, the three meditative stabilizations—initial preparation, supreme royal maṇḍala, and supreme royal activities
   - a middling divine approximation, which is the abbreviated generation rite and so forth of the supreme royal maṇḍala, or
   - a brief divine approximation, which is comprised of the great yoga together with a hundred thousand repetitions for each deity.
3. To confer initiation on others, perform the rite until obtaining permission from the deities.

If you have obtained a master's initiation but do not wish to bestow initiation on a student and merely wish to achieve your own deity, you must perform the great yoga of self-completion and cultivate the three meditative stabilizations in at least their brief form:

Great Yoga of Self-Completion

Bathe and so forth.
Generate, that is, imagine your basic body as Vajrasattva.
Imagine the whole maṇḍala in your own body.
In meditation receive full initiation.
Make offerings, and so forth.
Meditate in the pattern of the production of very pure phenomena, mimicking the pattern of Bodhisattvas' meditation in their last lifetime, as when Shākyamuni performed alternating and leap-over meditations prior to his full enlightenment. Imagine generating the four concentrations and four formless absorptions—limitless space, limitless

[a] *bdag rdzogs chen po'i rnal 'byor.*

consciousness, nothingness, and peak of cyclic existence—in forward order and then generate them in reverse order. Again ascend, but skip, for instance, the second concentration, leaping over levels of meditative stabilization. Finally, imitate the final step in becoming enlightened, the vajra-like meditative stabilization at the end of the continuum of being a sentient being who has obstructions yet to be abandoned.

Draw in the beings of bad transmigrations and remove the ill-deeds in their mental continuums.

Three Meditative Stabilizations

The extensive approximation is comprised by cultivating the three meditative stabilizations—initial preparation, supreme royal maṇḍala, and supreme royal activities—without omitting anything. The deities of the maṇḍala are emanated gradually in order:

- The central Vairochana emanates the sixteen male Bodhisattvas.
- The Ones-Gone-Thus in the four directions emanate the four female Bodhisattvas of the respective directions.
- Vairochana emanates the four offering goddesses.
- The Ones-Gone-Thus of the four directions emanate the four outer offering goddesses: Vajradhūpe, Vajrapuṣhpe, Vajrāloke, and Vajragandhe in series.
- The central Vairochana also emanates the four gate-keepers.

The middling approximation is an abbreviated form of the emanation of deities in the supreme royal maṇḍala; the Ones-Gone-Thus of the four directions emanate the deities of their particular quarter all at once.

The brief approximation requires just the great yoga of self-completion with one hundred thousand repetitions of the mantra of each deity of the maṇḍala.

Whether you wish to confer initiation on others or not, meditate every day in four sessions until the Vajra Element Great Maṇḍala is manifestly seen.

Procedure for Those Unable to Cultivate either the Yoga Observing a Single Deity or the Yoga Observing a Mandala of Deities

A procedure for practice is presented for those incapable of performing either of the above two types of deity meditation. This level, while not serving as a substitute for actual deity meditation, is a bottom-line requirement for conferring initiation, performing consecrations of images, and so forth:

Repeat only the essence-mantra of the deity and consider yourself to be the deity, even though you do not have clear imagination of such.

Pretend that such a deity is in front you and make offering, praise, and so forth.

Complete the prescribed count of mantra repetition.

This is a case of calling recitation of the ritual formulation of a deity yoga "meditation," even though it is not.

Yoga Observing a Subtle Hand-Symbol in Four Sessions

The purpose of meditating observing a subtle, or tiny, hand-symbol is to make the mind stable and then to develop dexterity of mind within that stability. The first part is to make the mind stable through observing a subtle object, which is done after deity yoga. Then:

Finish all activities.

Stay in an isolated place that is not noisy.

Straighten the body in a cross-legged posture.

Put the tongue from its root upward behind the upper teeth.

Put the two lips together.

Keep the eyes partly closed and aimed at the tip of the nose.

Keep the shoulders level.

Keep the head even, bent a little down, the nose in line with the navel.

Breathe quietly and gently.

Imagine a minute five-pointed vajra, of the same color as your deity—ranging in size from the most subtle, just the tip of a hair, to the largest, just a grain of sesame—standing at the tip of your nose and hold your mind on it. Or, first imagine it at your navel, and then upon saying *sūkṣmavajra* draw it up from there to the tip of the nose. Or, imagine it as rising from the heart region with the movement of the breath to the tip of the nose.

The subtle hand-symbol is like a stable post to which the wild elephant of the mind is tied through mindfulness and introspection. First visualize the object of observation; then generate a powerful intention to stay on the object, thinking, "My mind will be set on this object."

If your mind is too tight, excitement will be generated, and if too loose, laxity will be generated. You have to figure out yourself the middle ground free from both of these.

Stop exhalation and inhalation of breath, hold the breath in the nose, and concentrate on the subtle hand-symbol. In time, the subtle hand-symbol will become stable, and bliss will be generated at the tip of the nose or in another place in the body, making your body serviceable.

Physical pliancy generates mental pliancy, which here means calm abiding.

Meditate continuously for two months, dividing the day into four sessions. Single-pointed meditative stabilization—not interrupted by even subtle laxity and excitement—can be attained.

Then, to develop meditative dexterity by imagining the diffusion and gathering back of many tiny vajras:

Imagine the hand-symbol as pervading your body.

Saying *spharavajra* ("diffuse vajras"), scatter a multitude of vajras like wind blown on dust, causing them to pervade ever greater areas by degrees—a mile or two, then a hundred, then a thousand, then ten thousand, then a hundred thousand miles, then filling the billion worlds of this world system, and finally through the Desire, Form, and Formless Realms.

Saying *saṃharaṇavajra* ("gather vajras") and feeling breath being inhaled, withdraw the vajras back to the single vajra at the tip of your nose, where they become one vajra, and meditate on it.

At the end of the session, withdraw that single hand-symbol to your heart through the right nostril, and, placing it at the heart, make it stable, saying *oṃ dṛḍhatiṣṭha* ("oṃ stand firm").

In sum, first you achieve a fully qualified calm abiding by developing the factor of stability within meditating on a single tiny vajra. Then, when calm abiding—conjoined with physical and mental pliancy—is achieved, you train in diffusion and withdrawal again and again to develop meditative dexterity.

Yoga Without Signs

For the yoga without signs:

Meditate on yourself as a deity of one the four lineages, such as Vairochana.
Visualize in front of yourself a deity like yourself.
Contemplate mantra letters at the heart of the deity in front.
Ascertain that the deity that is yourself and the deity in front, as well as the mantra letters, are without inherent existence.

Understanding the meaning of the Sanskrit letter *a,* a negative, as the mere absence of inherent existence with respect to all phenomena, meditate by way of reasoning proving that all the mantras, letters, and deities are empty of inherent existence. Having been broken down, they do not appear. In conjunction with the wind yoga of stopping breath and distraction, when exhaling, let the breath out within experiencing the touch of subtle breath inside the nose, and contemplate the deity in front. Upon inhaling, stop breath and distraction, and contemplate emptiness without the appearance of any form to the ascertainment factor of the mind, even though the deity and so forth remain appearing to the appearance factor of the mind.

If your lineage is that of the One-Gone-Thus:
Meditate on yourself as having a body of a Buddha such as Vairochana.
Contemplate the letters of the mantra at the heart of similar deities meditated in front of you and filling space.
Ascertain the selflessness of persons and phenomena with respect to the deities—yourself and in front. When you gain ascertainment of their absence of inherent existence, the appearance of yourself and the deity in front vanish in the face of the ascertainment factor of the wisdom realizing emptiness even though they still appear to the appearance factor of that consciousness, except when emptiness is directly perceived. Concentrate single-pointedly on emptiness.

If yours is the vajra lineage:
Meditate on yourself as Vajrasattva.
Place the mantra letters in the center of vajras contemplated in front of yourself and filling the sky.
Ascertain the absence of inherent existence through individually taking apart form and so forth, and set your mind single-pointedly on that emptiness.

If yours is the jewel lineage:
Meditate on yourself as Vajraratnasambhava.
Contemplate the mantra letters in space in front of yourself.
Ascertain object and subject as equally not truly existent, and meditate on that emptiness single-pointedly.

If yours is the lotus lineage:
Meditate on yourself as Lokeshvara.
Set the mantra letters on lotuses filling the sky in front of yourself.
Ascertain all phenomena as not inherently existent, and meditate on that.

After intensively analyzing to determine whether the mantra letters and deities inherently exist and gaining improvement with respect to understanding the emptiness of inherent existence, stop analysis for the time being, and set the mind single-pointedly on the emptiness that you have understood. Before your mind becomes too settled, switch again to analytical meditation to revivify and heighten your understanding, and then switch back to stabilizing meditation, concentrating on the emptiness understood through analysis. By alternating this way between stabilizing and analytical meditation, eventually you will attain a natural equal operation of calm abiding and special insight without needing to apply antidotes to laxity and excitement—a union of calm abiding and special insight.

Appendix: *Achieving Buddhahood through the Five Manifest Enlightenments*
by Lo-sang-chö-ḡyi-gyel-tsen

from the First Paṇchen Lama L̄o-sang-chö-ḡyi-gyel-tsen's
Notes on a Presentation of the General Teaching and the Tantra Sets[185]

Question: Then how is the fruit [Buddhahood] actualized in dependence on this path?

Answer: Even though there are many different assertions on this by the three masters expert in Yoga [Tantra—namely, Buddhaguhya, Shākyamitra, and Ānandagarbha], let us condense the essence of our own system. Either you progress over the ten grounds in dependence upon the paths and supreme feat explained earlier, or [you actualize enlightenment the way] the great Bodhisattva Sarvārthasiddhi did. He progressed over the ten grounds of the path of the Perfection Vehicle itself, and then in his last lifetime was dwelling in meditative equipoise in the meditative stabilization pervading space in the Heavily Adorned Highest Pure Land in the essence [or best] of places—like, for example, the essence of butters—called the essence of enlightenment. The Conquerors, filling the sphere of space like [sesame seeds filling] a sesame pod, roused him from meditative stabilization with the sound of their snapping fingers and "*oṃ vajra uttiṣṭha,*" whereupon they said:

> O child of good lineage, without actualizing the principles of all Buddhas you cannot become buddhafied merely through this.[a]

Then, seeing them vividly and hearing their speech, he bowed down with "*oṃ sarvatathāgata-vandanaṃ karomi*" ("I make homage to all Ones-Gone-Thus.") and asked, "Please indicate those principles which, if not actualized,[186] Buddhahood is not attained."

---

[a] The *Compendium of Principles Tantra* itself says:

> Child of good lineage, how will you complete the unsurpassed complete and perfect enlightenment, you who act with energy for all austerities without the knowledge of the principles of all Ones-Gone-Thus?

Adapted from the translation by Steven Weinberger.

1. Due to this the Conquerors, having first bestowed the crown initiation and so forth, said:

> O child of good family, repeat this naturally established mantra *citta-prativedhaṃ karomi* ("I experience the mind.") Manifestly realize the suchness of your mind.

The Bodhisattva contemplated and analyzed the meaning of the mantra, whereby he actualized the suchness of his own mind, the sixteen emptinesses, which are the emptinesses of the two selves—of persons and of phenomena. Subsequent to meditative equipoise he directly saw the object of apprehension, emptiness, in the aspect of a moon disc dwelling at his own heart, and he said to the Buddhas, "It is thus." This is enlightenment from individual clear realization of the mind—the first manifest enlightenment. At that time, the Bodhisattva attained the entity of the mirror-like wisdom, the nature of Akṣhobhya.

As a practice for followers, it is taught that [the sixteen vowels which symbolize][187] the sixteen emptinesses transform into a moon disc generated [at your heart].[188]

2. Furthermore, the Buddhas said:

> Child of good lineage, like transforming a white cloth with dye, as much as you train in the naturally clear light that is the suchness of your own mind, so much does it become pure, and the mind of enlightenment is transformed into higher and higher increase.[a] Therefore, take to mind the meaning of this naturally established mantra "*oṃ bodhicittaṃ utpādayāmi*" ("*Oṃ* I generate the mind of enlightenment.") and cultivate the mind of enlightenment.

Moreover, when he had meditated that way, in meditative equipoise he directly realized the naturally clear suchness of his own mind, the suchness purified also of adventitious defilements. Subsequent to meditative equipoise he saw the wisdom realizing emptiness as a second moon on the moon that is the object of apprehension [that is, as a second moon on top of the moon that is emptiness]. At that time he attained the entity of Ratnasambhava's exalted wisdom of equality.

---

[a] The *Compendium of Principles Tantra* itself says:

> Child of good lineage, since this mind is naturally luminous, as it is cultivated, so does it become. It is like, for example, dyeing a white cloth with dye.

Adapted from the translation by Steven Weinberger.

When this is practiced by followers, it is taught that a second moon is to be generated from the consonants that symbolize thoroughly complete abandonment [of defilements] and realization [of selflessness]—a state devoid of adventitious defilements.

3. Furthermore, the Buddhas said:

> Child of good lineage, in order to make stable that thoroughly good mind of enlightenment, take cognizance of it as the vajra element and blissfully repeat this naturally established mantra "*oṃ tiṣṭha-vajra*" ("stable vajra").

Moreover, through thinking on and contemplating the meaning of that mantra, in meditative equipoise even the dualistic appearance that was the appearance of a moon vanished, and he actualized suchness [in direct perception]. Subsequent [to meditative equipoise the emptiness that is] the object of apprehension of that exalted wisdom turned into the aspect of a five-pointed vajra, which he saw set on the moon at his heart. This is the third manifest enlightenment, called "being enlightened from the stable[189] vajra."

4. Then, that great being said, "The meaning is thus," whereupon all the Ones-Gone-Thus caused all the potencies of the exalted body, speech, and mind vajras of the Buddhas to enter into the vajra at the heart of that Conqueror Child [that is, Bodhisattva] and blessed him into magnificence, saying:

> Take to mind the meaning of this naturally established mantra "*vajra-ātmako 'ham*" ("Having a vajra nature am I.") and cultivate the mind of enlightenment.

Moreover, through having cultivated such he saw his own body as an exalted body having the nature of vajras established from the minute particles of all Ones-Gone-Thus. Having been apprised of that fact, all the Buddhas also conferred on that Bodhisattva the initiation of the name "Vajradhātu" (Vajra Element). *Dhātu* is used for the two, constituent and cause; hence, to summarize the meaning, the name was given to mean that the capacity for that Conqueror Child quickly to turn into the body of the Supramundane Victor Mahāvairochana was complete. This is the transformation into the entity of the exalted wisdom of achieving activities, which has the nature of Amoghasiddhi. It is the fourth manifest enlightenment, called "enlightenment from the vajra essence."

5. Then he said, "[My] body having the nature of the vajra element is like a vajra," whereupon the Buddhas said:

> Child of good lineage, repeat this naturally established mantra *oṃ yathā sarvatathāgatās tathā 'haṃ* ("As all the Ones-Gone-Thus are, so am I."), and meditate on your own body as the great seal of exalted body of all the Buddhas.

Then, all the Ones-Gone-Thus in the aspects of the respective deities dissolved into the vajra at the heart of the Bodhisattva Vajradhātu, whereby he was blessed into magnificence. In the next moment, the Bodhisattva Vajradhātu was buddhafied as the Complete Enjoyment Body of Vairochana—the entity of the exalted wisdom of the element of attributes—with a white body, one face, and two arms, with the hand-configuration of supreme enlightenment, and having a nature of the complete signs [of a Buddha body]. This is the fifth manifest enlightenment, called "enlightenment in exact accordance with all Buddhas without exception."

The master Ānandagarbha's explanation in such a serial way is relative to the practice of followers. For when on the occasion of the fruit [of Buddhahood] the first manifest enlightenment has been actualized, the remaining manifest enlightenments also have been actualized because, as is said, the five exalted wisdoms are one entity and different isolates.

In that way, most Indian and Tibetan scholars assert that the original Complete Enjoyment Body is Vairochana with one face and two arms and that Vairochana with four faces is an Emanation Body emanated by him. One who has been buddhafied as such a Complete Enjoyment Body creates the four types of miracles—the miracle of magnificent blessing, the miracle of conferring initiation, the miracle of meditative stabilization, and the miracle of exalted activity.

Furthermore, since the terminology of "manifest enlightenments" does not occur in action and performance tantras, the manifest enlightenments are distinguishing features of the two higher tantra sets [Yoga and Highest Yoga]. Furthermore, although the names are similar in those two, the meaning is totally different, due to which they differ greatly.

Backnotes

[1] H.H. the Dalai Lama, Tsong-ka-pa, and Jeffrey Hopkins, *Tantra in Tibet* (London: George Allen and Unwin, 1977; reprint, with minor corrections, Ithaca, N.Y.: Snow Lion, 1987).

[2] Ibid., 120-121.

[3] Ibid., 122-128.

[4] Ibid., 129, 134.

[5] Ibid., 129-130.

[6] Ibid., 130.

[7] Ibid., 130.

[8] Ibid., 131.

[9] Ibid., 131.

[10] Ibid., 131-132.

[11] Ibid., 143-150.

[12] H.H. the Dalai Lama, Tsong-ka-pa, and Jeffrey Hopkins, *The Yoga of Tibet* (London: George Allen and Unwin, 1981; reprinted as *Deity Yoga* with minor corrections, Ithaca: Snow Lion, 1987).

[13] *Extensive General Presentation of the Tantra Sets*, Collected Works Part 15 *ba*, 86.6-88.7.

[14] Ibid., 54.5-61.7.

[15] *Deity Yoga*, 48-49.

[16] *vairocanābhisambodhitantrapiṇḍārtha, rnam par snang mdzad mngon par rdzogs par byang chub pa'i rgyud kyi bsdus pa'i don;* P3486, vol. 77; Buddhaguhya also wrote a longer *Explanation* of the same tantra, *vairocanābhisambodhivikurvitādhiṣṭhānamahātantrabhāṣya, rnam par snang mdzad mngon par byang chub pa rnam par sprul pa'i byin gyis brlabs kyi rgyud chen po'i bshad pa;* P3487, vol.77, p. 110, *rgyud 'grel, ngu* 76b.8-337a.3; D2663, *rgyud, nyu* 65a.3-260b.7; and *vairocanābhisambodhivikurvitādhiṣṭhānamahātantravṛtti, rnam par snang mdzad mngon par byang chub pa rnam par sprul pa'i byin gyis brlabs kyi rgyud chen po'i 'grel pa;* P3490, vol.77, p. 229, *rgyud 'grel, cu* 1-230a.5; D2663, *rgyud, nyu* 261a.1-*tu* 116a.7.

[17] *de bzhin gshegs pa thams cad kyi de kho na nyid bsdus pa, sarvatathāgatatattvasaṃgraha;* P112, vol. 4; Toh. 479, vol. *nya.*

[18] *gsang ba rnal 'byor chen po'i rgyud rdo rje rtse mo, vajraśekharamahāguhyayogatantra;* P113, vol. 5; Toh. 480, vol. *nya.*

[19] P3324, vol. 70. Ḏzong-ka-ḇa cites Padmavajra's *Commentarial Explanation of (Buddhaguhya's) "Introduction to the Meaning of the Tantra"* (*rgyud kyi don la 'jug pa'i 'grel bshad, tantrārthāvatāravyākhyāna;* P3325, vol. 70; Toh. 2502, vol. *'i*, 242a.5) a few times.

[20] *de kho na nyid snang ba, tattvālokakāri;* P3333, vols. 71-72; Toh. 2510, vol. *li.*

[21] The longer is *rdo rje sems dpa' 'byung ba zhes bya ba'i sgrub thabs, vajrasattvodayanāmasādhana,* P3340, vol. 74, 29.3.5; and the shorter is *rdo rje sems dpa'i sgrub pa'i thabs, vajrasattvasādhana,* P3341, vol. 74, 31.5.4-31.5.8.

[22] *rdo rje dbyings kyi dkyil 'khor chen po'i cho ga rdo rje thams cad 'byung ba, vajradhātumhāmaṇḍalopāyikasarvavajrodaya;* P3339, vol. 74; Toh. 2516, vol. *ku,* 43a-44a. This text is often referred to as *rdo rje thams cad 'byung ba* (*sarvavajrodaya*) or *rdo rje 'byung ba* (*vajrodaya*).

[23] *dpal mchog dang po'i rgya cher bshad pa, śrīparamādyaṭīkā;* P3335, vols. 72-73; Toh. 2512, vol. *si.*

[24] *de kho na nyid bsdus pa'i rgya cher bshad pa ko sa la'i rgyan, tattvasaṃgrahaṭīkākosalālaṃkāra;* P3326, vols. 70-71; Toh. 2503, vol. *yi,* 154a.7-154b.2.

[25] *dpal mchog dang po zhes bya ba theg pa chen po'i rtog pa'i rgyal po, śrīparamādyanāmamahāyānakalparāja;* P119, vol. 5; Toh. 488, vol. *ta.*

[26] *de bzhin gshegs pa thams cad kyi de kho na nyid bsdus pa, sarvatathāgatatattvasaṃgraha;* P112, vol. 4; Toh. 479, vol. *nya.*

[27] *gsang ba rnal 'byor chen po'i rgyud rdo rje rtse mo, vajraśekharamahāguhyayogatantra;* P113, vol. 5; Toh. 480, vol. *nya.*

[28] *shes rab kyi pha rol tu phyin pa'i man ngag gi bstan bcos mngon par rtogs pa'i rgyan, abhisamayālaṃkāra-prajñāpāramitopadeśaśāstra,* P5184, vol. 88; Toh. 3786.

[29] *dpal mchog dang po'i rgya cher bshad pa, śrīparamādyaṭīkā;* P3335, vols. 72-73; Toh. 2512, vols. *si-'i.*

[30] *de bzhin gshegs pa thams cad kyi sku gsung thugs kyi gsang chen gsang ba 'dus pa zhes bya ba brtag pa'i rgyal po chen po, sarvatathāgatakāyavākcittarahasyaguhyasamājanāmamahākalparāja;* P81, vol. 3; Toh. 442, vol. *ca;* Dharma vol. 29.

[31] In the text read *ni* for *na.*

[32] Karmapa *sde dge* version of *Tattvasaṃgraha,* 136a.1. (Thanks to Steven Weinberger for the

note.)

33 *rgyud kyi don la 'jug pa, tantrārthāvatāra;* P3324, vol. 70.

34 *rdo rje thams cad 'byung ba'i rgya cher bshad pa yid bzhin nor bu;* Collected Works, vol. 11.

35 *sgom pa'i rim pa, bhāvanākrama,* P5310-5312, vol. 102; Toh. 3915-3917, vol. *ki.*

36 *lam rim chen mo,* P6001, vol. 152 and *lam rim chung ngu,* P6002, vol. 152.

37 *rgyud kyi don la 'jug pa, tantrārthāvatāra,* P3324, vol. 70; Toh. 2501, vol. *'i.*

38 *Commentarial Explanation of (Buddhaguhya's) "Introduction to the Meaning of the Tantra" (rgyud kyi don la 'jug pa'i 'grel bshad, tantrārthāvatāravyākhyāna*); P3325, vol. 70; Toh. 2502, vol. *'i.*

39 Dzong-ka-ba Lo-sang-drak-ba (*tsong kha pa blo bzang grags pa,* 1357-1419), *Great Exposition of Secret Mantra / The Stages of the Path to a Conqueror and Pervasive Master, a Great Vajradhara: Revealing All Secret Topics (rgyal ba khyab bdag rdo rje 'chang chen po'i lam gyi rim pa gsang ba kun gyi gnad rnam par phye ba*), P6210, vol. 161; for other editions see Bibliography.

40 *de kho na nyid bsdus pa, tattvasaṃgraha;* P112, vol. 4, Toh. 479, vol. *nya.*

41 Ke-drup Ge-lek-bel-sang (*mkhas grub dge legs dpal bzang,* 1385-1438), *Extensive Expression of the Presentation of the General Tantra Sets (rgyud sde spyi'i rnam par gzhag pa rgyas par brjod pa*), 216.11. The edition used is that published by Ferdinand D. Lessing and Alex Wayman, *Mkhas Grub Rje's Fundamentals of the Buddhist Tantras* (The Hague: Mouton, 1968; reprint, Delhi: Motilal Banarsidass, 1978), hereafter referred to as "Ke-drup's *Fundamentals.*"

42 Buddhaguhya's *Introduction to the Meaning of the Tantra,* P3324, vol. 70, 39.4.5. See Bu-dön's *Extensive Explanation of (Ānandagarbha's) "Source of All Vajras": Wish-Granting Jewel (rdo rje thams cad 'byung ba'i rgya cher bshad pa yid bzhin nor bu*), in Collected Works, vol. 11, 269.7.

43 Ke-drup's *Fundamentals,* 216.22.

44 Ibid., 218.1.

45 Ibid., 218.3. I have added "of deity yoga" for the sake of clarity.

46 Ibid., 218.4.

47 Ibid., 218.6.

48 Ibid., 218.7.

49 See H.H. the Dalai Lama, Tsong-ka-pa, and Jeffrey Hopkins, *Tantra in Tibet* (London: George Allen and Unwin, 1977; reprint, with minor corrections, Ithaca, N.Y.: Snow Lion, 1987), 163, second paragraph.

50 *dpal mchog dang po'i rgya cher bshad pa, śrīparamādyaṭīkā;* P3335, vols. 72-73; Toh. 2512, vol. *si,* 50a.5, 50b.4, 51a.3, 51b.2. See Bu-dön's *Extensive Explanation of (Ānandagarbha's) "Source of All Vajras": Wish-Granting Jewel,* in Collected Works, vol. 11, 267.7-268.6.

51 Ke-drup's *Fundamentals,* 220.10.

52 Ibid., 220.10.

53 The final sentence is drawn from ibid., 222.12.

54 Ibid., 222.16.

55 Ibid., 224.7.

56 Ibid., 224.6.

57 Ibid., 224.9.

58 Ibid., 224.4.

59 P3324, vol. 70, 36.5.1-37.5.1. Ke-drup's *Fundamentals* does not cite this passage.

60 *de kho na nyid snang ba, tattvālokakārī;* P3333, vols. 71-72; Toh. 2510, vol. *li.*

61 P3324, vol. 70, 39.5.2-39.5.6. This paragraph and quote are not in Ke-drup's *Fundamentals.* Lessing and Wayman give Buddhaguhya's explanation in a footnote (*Fundamentals,* 224, n. 20).

62 P3324, vol. 70, 39.5.6-39.5.8. This passage follows the previous quote.

63 This paragraph and the next are not in Ke-drup's *Fundamentals.*

64 This question and answer are not in Ke-drup's *Fundamentals.*

65 This paragraph is found in Ke-drup's *Fundamentals* (227); the remainder of Dzong-ka-ba's section on Yoga Tantra is not in Ke-drup's *Fundamentals.*

66 *rtsa ltung gi rnam bshad / gsang sngags kyi tshul khrims kyi rnam bshad dngos grub kyi snye ma zhes bya ba,* P6188, vol. 160. For an excellent complete translation, see Gareth Sparham, *An Explanation of Tantric Morality Called "Fruit Cluster of Siddhis"* (Wisdom Publications: forthcoming).

67 P3324, vol. 70, 38.2.5-38.3.1.

68 *dpal mchog dang po, śrīparamādya;* P120, vol. 5; Toh. 488, vol. *ta,* 228a.3.

69 *gsang ba rnal 'byor chen po'i rgyud rdo rje rtse mo, vajraśekharamahāguhyayogatantra;* P113, vol. 5; Toh. 480, vol. *nya,* 183a.

70 Toh. 480, vol. *nya,* 199b.1-199b.3. Quoted in Buddhaguhya's *Introduction to the Meaning of*

the Tantra, P3324, vol. 70, 50.5.2, and by Bu-d̄ön in his *Condensed General Presentation of the Tantra Sets,* in Collected Works, vol. 14, 880.7.

71 Toh. 2510, vol. *li,* 148a.7-148b.5.

72 For corresponding section, see Bu-d̄ön's *Explanation,* 314.7-316.4.

73 Ibid., 326.2.

74 The longer is *rdo rje sems dpa' 'byung ba zhes bya ba'i sgrub thabs, vajrasattvodayanāmasādhana,* P3340, vol. 74, 29.3.5; and the shorter is *rdo rje sems dpa'i sgrub pa'i thabs, vajrasattvasādhana,* P3341, vol. 74, 31.5.4-31.5.8.

75 P3340, vol. 74, 29.4.2. D̄zong-ka-b̄a adds a few words to what is otherwise almost verbatim.

76 Bu-d̄ön's *Practice of (Ānandagarbha's) "Rite of the Vajra Element [Great] Maṇḍala: Source of All Vajras": Wish-Fulfilling Gem,* in Collected Works, vol. 12, 233.6-233.7, gives detail: *mthe bong dang gung mos se gol brdeb pa rdo rje bsdu ba'i phyag rgya dang / badzra sama dzaḥ zhes brjod pas / skad cig tsam la zhing rab 'byams nas de bzhin gshegs pa rang rang gi 'khor byang chub sems dpa'i tshogs dang bcas pa dpag tu med pa bsdus pas /.*

77 P3341, vol. 74, 31.5.8.

78 P3340, vol. 74, 29.4.3.

79 Toh. 2510, vol. *li,* 151b.4.

80 Toh. 2510, vol. *li,* 151b.3. This passage is cited in Bu-d̄ön's *Condensed General Presentation of the Tantra Sets,* vol. 14, 882.5.

81 The bracketed material is from the Dalai Lama, based on Ānandagarbha's *Extensive Explanation of the "Shrīparamādya Tantra"* (*dpal mchog dang po'i rgya cher bshad pa, śrīparamādyaṭīkā;* P3335, vols. 72-73; Toh. 2512, vols. *si-'i*). Ānandagarbha goes on to explain that all-yoga (*thams cad rnal 'byor*) is to meditate on the nature of all animate and inanimate phenomena and that intense yoga (*shin tu rnal 'byor*) is to meditate single-pointedly on the content of the above three yogas—yoga, subsequent yoga, and all-yoga.

82 P3340, vol. 74, 30.2.2.

83 Toh. 2510, vol. *li,* 2a.4. This passage is cited in Bu-d̄ön's *Condensed General Presentation of the Tantra Sets,* vol. 14, 882.1.

84 Toh. 2516, vol. *ku,* 22b.2.

85 Toh. 2510, vol. *li,* 148a.6.

86 See Buddhaguhya's *Introduction to the Meaning of the Tantra,* P3324, vol. 70, 52.1.2.

87 Buddhaguhya's *Introduction to the Meaning of the Tantra,* P3324, vol. 70, 46.2.1-46.3.5.

88 Ibid., 46.3.5-46.3.8.

89 This section corresponds to Bu-d̄ön's *Condensed General Presentation of the Tantra Sets,* vol. 14, 883.1-883.5.

90 Buddhaguhya's *Introduction to the Meaning of the Tantra,* P3324, vol. 70, 51.4.7.

91 Ibid., 51.5.1. This passage immediately follows the preceding quote.

92 *Compendium of Principles Tantra,* Karmapa Derge edition, 127b.5-127b.6.

93 Toh. 2510, vol. *li,* 200a.6.

94 Buddhaguhya's *Introduction to the Meaning of the Tantra,* P3324, vol. 70, 52.1.6.

95 Ibid., 51.5.8.

96 Ibid., 52.1.3.

97 Toh. 2510, vol. *li,* 200b.2.

98 Toh. 2503, vol. *yi,* 155b.2.

99 Buddhaguhya's *Introduction to the Meaning of the Tantra,* P3324, vol. 70, 52.1.5.

100 Toh. 2503, vol. *yi,* 154b.4.

101 *dbu ma'i snying po, madhyamakahṛdaya,* P5255, vol. 96, 4.1.7.

102 Toh. 2503, vol. *yi,* 154b.1.

103 Toh. 2503, vol. *yi,* 154b.6-155a.1.

104 Perhaps, his *Compendium of Ascertainments* (*rnal 'byor spyod pa'i sa dbab pa bsdu ba, yogacaryābhumi-viniścaya-saṃgrahaṇī;* Toh. 4038, vol. *zi*), 67b.1.

105 Toh. 2510, vol. *li,* 200b.3.

106 Toh. 2510, vol. *li,* 200a.3.

107 P3324, vol. 70, 52.2.4.

108 Following the Peking edition reading of Buddhaguhya's text (P3324, vol. 70, 52.3.1).

109 Toh. 2503, vol. *yi,* 155b.2.

110 The Peking edition of Buddhaguhya's *Introduction to the Meaning of the Tantra* (P3324, vol. 70, 52.3.2) reads the same.

111 Toh. 2510, vol. *li,* 200a.5-200b.5.

112 *gsang ba 'dus pa, guhyasamāja;* P81, vol. 3; Toh. 442, vol. *ca.*

113 In this section, D̄zong-ka-b̄a follows the exposition in Buddhaguhya's *Introduction to the Meaning of the Tantra* (P3324, vol. 70, 62.1.1-63.1.1) with the exception of one sentence and the last paragraph, which are his own.

114 D479, vol. *nya,* 134b.2. Bu-d̄ön, in his *Condensed General Presentation of the Tantra Sets* (Collected Works, vol. 14, 884.7 and 885.2), quotes the first two stanzas. The first stanza is cited in Buddhaguhya's *Introduction to the Meaning of the Tantra,* P3324, vol. 70, 62.2.4.

[115] The sources for the brackets are Buddhaguhya's and Ḍzong-ka-ḃa's commentaries; see below.

[116] Buddhaguhya's *Introduction to the Meaning of the Tantra,* P3324, vol. 70, 62.2.4-62.4.3.

[117] Ḍzong-ka-ḃa is paraphrasing Buddhaguhya's *Introduction to the Meaning of the Tantra,* P3324, vol. 70, 62.4.3-62.5.3.

[118] Buddhaguhya's *Introduction to the Meaning of the Tantra,* P3324, vol. 70, 62.4.4.

[119] This sentence is not in Buddhaguhya's *Introduction to the Meaning of the Tantra.*

[120] Ḍzong-ka-ḃa is paraphrasing Buddhaguhya's *Introduction to the Meaning of the Tantra,* P3324, vol. 70, 62.5.3-62.5.6.

[121] Ḍzong-ka-ḃa is paraphrasing ibid., 62.5.6-62.5.8.

[122] Ḍzong-ka-ḃa is paraphrasing ibid., 63.1.4-63.2.3.

[123] Toh. 480, vol. *nya,* 160b.7-161a.4.

[124] Ḍzong-ka-ḃa is paraphrasing Buddhaguhya's *Introduction to the Meaning of the Tantra,* P3324, vol. 70, 63.2.3-63.2.7.

[125] Toh. 480, vol. *nya,* 161a.4-161b.1.

[126] Ḍzong-ka-ḃa is paraphrasing Buddhaguhya's *Introduction to the Meaning of the Tantra,* P3324, vol. 70, 63.2.7-63.3.4.

[127] Toh. 480, vol. *nya,* 161b.1-161b.4.

[128] Ḍzong-ka-ḃa is paraphrasing Buddhaguhya's *Introduction to the Meaning of the Tantra,* P3324, vol. 70, 63.3.4.

[129] Toh. 480, vol. *nya,* 161b.4.

[130] Buddhaguhya's *Introduction to the Meaning of the Tantra,* P3324, vol. 70, 62.1.1.

[131] Toh. 2503, vol. *yi,* 3b.5.

[132] Toh. 2503, vol. *yi,* 3b.6-4a.1.

[133] Buddhaguhya's *Introduction to the Meaning of the Tantra,* P3324, vol. 70, 62.1.3.

[134] In his *Condensed General Presentation of the Tantra Sets* (Collected Works, vol. 14, 884.3-884.7), Bu-ḋön paraphrases this same material (Buddhaguhya's *Introduction to the Meaning of the Tantra,* P3324, vol. 70, 62.1.6) but in the context of those who cannot meditate.

[135] P3340, vol. 74, 29.4.2. See 85.

[136] Chapter eighteen of the *Guhyasamāja Tantra;* Toh. 442, vol. *ca,* 154a.4; Sanskrit text edited by S. Bagchi, *Guhyasamāja Tantra* (Darbhanga, India: The Mithila Institute, 1965), 132.

[137] *sgom rim, bhāvanākrama,* P5310-5312, vol. 102. The second of these three texts has been translated by Geshe Lhundup Sopa, Elvin W. Jones, and John Newman, *The Stages of Meditation: Bhāvanākrama II* (Madison, WI: Deer Park Books, 1998) and by Geshe Lobsang Jordhen, Lobsang Choephel Ganchenpa, and Jeremy Russell, *Stages of Meditation* (Ithaca, NY: Snow Lion Publications, 2001).

[138] *shes rab kyi pha rol tu phyin pa'i man ngag, prajñāpāramitopadeśa,* P5798, vol. 114.

[139] See Tsong-kha-pa, *The Great Treatise on the Stages of the Path to Enlightenment,* vol. 3, trans. and ed. Joshua W. C. Cutler and Guy Newland (Ithaca, N.Y.: Snow Lion, 2002), Part One.

[140] Buddhaguhya's *Introduction to the Meaning of the Tantra,* P3324, vol. 70, 69.3.7.

[141] Ibid., 68.2.5.

[142] Ibid., 68.2.6.

[143] This and the next paragraph paraphrase Buddhaguhya's *Introduction to the Meaning of the Tantra,* P3324, vol. 70, 52.3.8ff.

[144] Ibid., 53.1.8.

[145] *Compendium of Principles,* Toh. 479, vol. *nya,* 28b.6-28b.7.

[146] Ibid., 28b.7.

[147] This paragraph paraphrases Buddhaguhya's *Introduction to the Meaning of the Tantra,* P3324, vol. 70, 53.4.2.

[148] The paragraph paraphrases Buddhaguhya (P3324, vol. 70, 54.2.6), who also gives an alternate method (54.2.8).

[149] This paragraph paraphrases ibid., 54.1.5.

[150] Bu-ḋön's *Practice of (Ānandagarbha's) "Rite of the Vajra Element [Great] Maṇḍala: Source of All Vajras": Wish-Fulfilling Gem,* vol. 12, 314.3, and Buddhaguhya's *Introduction to the Meaning of the Tantra,* P3324, vol. 70, 54.2.6.

[151] Buddhaguhya's *Introduction to the Meaning of the Tantra,* 54.1.6.

[152] This paragraph paraphrases ibid., 57.1.6-57.2.6.

[153] Ibid., 54.4.4.

[154] Ibid., 57.5.6.

[155] Oral commentary from Lati Rin-ḃo-chay.

[156] Paraphrasing ibid., 64.4.6-64.4.8.

[157] The sub-headings have been added for clarity. This section paraphrases ibid., 64.5.4-65.1.2.

[158] Paraphrasing ibid., 65.1.3-65.2.2.

[159] Buddhaguhya does not mention "on top of your head."

[160] Buddhaguhya does not mention "just raising it up."

[161] Buddhaguhya does not mention "at the point between your eyes."

[162] Buddhaguhya does not mention "at your heart."

[163] Paraphrasing ibid., 65.2.8-65.3.2. Much of the detail in this and the next sub-heading are not in Buddhaguhya even though the general run of the description is.

[164] Paraphrasing ibid., 65.3.2-65.3.3.

[165] Paraphrasing ibid., 65.3.3-65.3.4.

[166] Paraphrasing ibid., 65.3.7-65.4.4.

[167] Paraphrasing ibid., 65.4.4-65.4.7.

[168] Paraphrasing ibid., 65.2.3-65.2.8.

[169] Ibid., 59.2.4.

[170] Ibid., 59.4.1.

[171] Ibid., 60.2.5-60.3.2.

[172] Ibid., 59.3.2.

[173] Ibid., 61.1.7-61.2.2.

[174] Ibid., 61.1.5-61.3.2.

[175] This chapter on the five manifest enlightenments is from Ke-drup-ge-lek-b̄el-sang (*mkhas grub dge legs dpal bzang,* 1385-1438), *Extensive Explanation of the Format of the General Tantra Sets* (*rgyud sde spyi'i rnam par bzhag pa rgyas par bshad pa*), in Collected Works of the Lord Mkhas-grub rje dge-legs-dpal-bzaṅ-po, vol. 8 (New Delhi: Guru Deva, 1980), 449.5-455.3. See also the translation in Lessing and Wayman, *Fundamentals of the Buddhist Tantras,* Chapter One.

[176] Ke-drup-ge-lek-b̄el-sang, *Extensive Explanation of the Format of the General Tantra Sets,* in Collected Works of the Lord Mkhas-grub rje dge-legs-dpal-bzaṅ-po, vol. 8 (New Delhi: Guru Deva, 1980), 572.1-582.2. Also: Lessing and Wayman, *Fundamentals of the Buddhist Tantras,* 228.1-249.11.

[177] This bullet and the next are missing in the Guru Deva edition, 573.6.

[178] Ke-drup omits the three for the action seal, which are drawn from Paṇ-chen S̄ö-nam-drak-b̄a's (*paṇ chen bsod nams grags pa,* 1478-1554), *General Presentation of the Tantra Sets: Captivating the Minds of the Fortunate* (*rgyud sde spyi'i rnam par bzhag pa skal bzang gi yid 'phrog*) (Dharamsala: Library of Tibetan Works and Archives, 1975), 54.3-54.6.

[179] Toh. 480, vol. *nya,* 185b.6.

[180] Bracketed material is drawn from Ke-drup's *Fundamentals,* 238.13-238.23.

[181] *dbu ma la 'jug pa, madhyamakāvatāra;* XII.8d; *Toh.* 3861, vol. *'a,* 216b.3; Louis de la Vallée Poussin, *Madhyamakāvatāra par Candrakīrti,* Bibliotheca Buddhica 9 (Osnabrück, Germany: Biblio Verlag, 1970), 361.

[182] *rdo rje dbyings kyi dkyil 'khor chen po'i cho ga rdo rje thams cad 'byung ba, vajradhātu-mahāmaṇḍalopāyika sarva-vajrodaya;* P3339, vol. 74; Toh. 2516, vol. *ku.*

[183] Toh. 488, vol. *ta,* 264b.7-265a.1.

[184] *dpal mchog dang po'i rgya cher bshad pa, śrīparamādyaṭīkā;* P3335, vols. 72-73; Toh. 2512, vols. *si-'i.*

[185] Lo-sang-chö-ḡyi-gyel-tsen (*blo bzang chos kyi rgyal mtshan,* 1567[?]-1662), *Notes on a Presentation of the General Teaching and the Tantra Sets* (*bstan pa spyi dang rgyud sde bzhi'i rnam par bzhag pa'i zin bris*), in Collected Works, vol. 4 (New Delhi: Gurudeva, 1973), 71.3-76.2.

[186] *sngon* emended to *mngon,* as it appears at 71.6.

[187] Ke-drup's *Fundamentals,* 28.21.

[188] Ibid., 30.1.

[189] *bstan* emended to *brtan,* in accordance with ibid., 30.20.

List of Abbreviations

"Dharma" refers to the *sde dge* edition of the Tibetan canon published by Dharma Press: the *Nying-ma Edition of the sDe-dge bKa'-'gyur and bsTan-'gyur* (Oakland, Calif.: Dharma, 1980).

"Karmapa *sde dge*" refers to the *sde dge mtshal par bka' 'gyur: A Facsimile Edition of the 18th Century Redaction of Si tu chos kyi 'byung gnas Prepared under the Direction of H.H. the 16th rgyal dbang karma pa* (Delhi: Delhi Karmapae Chodhey Gyalwae Sungrab Partun Khang, 1977).

"P," standing for "Peking edition," refers to the *Tibetan Tripiṭaka* (Tokyo-Kyoto: Tibetan Tripiṭaka Research Foundation, 1955-1962).

"Toh" refers to the *Complete Catalogue of the Tibetan Buddhist Canons,* edited by Prof. Hukuji Ui (Sendai, Japan: Tohoku University, 1934), and *A Catalogue of the Tohuku University Collection of Tibetan Works on Buddhism,* edited by Prof. Yensho Kanakura (Sendai, Japan: Tohoku University, 1953).

"Tokyo *sde dge*" refers to the *sDe dge Tibetan Tripiṭaka—bsTan ḥgyur preserved at the Faculty of Letters, University of Tokyo,* edited by Z. Yamaguchi, et al. (Tokyo: Tokyo University Press, 1977-1984).

Bibliography

Sūtras and tantras are listed alphabetically by English title in the first section of the bibliography. Indian and Tibetan treatises are listed alphabetically by author in the second section.

1. Sutras and Tantras

Compendium of Principles Tantra (the root Yoga Tantra)
sarvatathāgatatattvasaṃgraha
de bzhin gshegs pa thams cad kyi de kho na nyid bsdus pa
P112, vol. 4; Toh. 479, vol. *nya*
Sanskrit: *Sarva-tathāgata-tattva-saṅgraha: Facsimile Reproduction of a Tenth Century Sanskrit Manuscript from Nepal,* reproduced by Lokesh Chandra and David L. Snellgrove. Śata-piṭaka Series, vol. 269. New Delhi: International Academy of Indian Culture, 1981. Also: Isshi Yamada. *Sarva-tathāgata-tattva-saṅgraha nāma mahāyāna-sūtra: A Critical Edition Based on the Sanskrit Manuscript and Chinese and Tibetan Translations.* Śata-piṭaka Series, vol. 262. New Delhi: International Academy of Indian Culture, 1981. Also: Kanjin Horiuchi, ed. *Shoe Kongōchōkyō no Kenkyū, Bonpon Kōteihen Bonzōkan Taishō,* vols. 1 & 2. Kōyasan University: Mikkyō Bunka Kenkyūjo, 1983.
Translation: Rolf W. Giebel. *Two Esoteric Sutras: The Adamantine Pinnacle Sutra; The Susiddhikara Sutra.* Berkeley, CA: Numata Center for Buddhist Translation and Research, 2001; *Adamantine Pinnacle Sutra* (= chapter 1 of *Tattvasaṅgraha*), 1-107; *Susiddhikara Sutra,* 109-325.

Guhyasamāja Tantra (a root Highest Yoga Tantra)
sarvatathāgatakāyavākcittarahasyaguhyasamājanāmamahākalparāja
de bzhin gshegs pa thams cad kyi sku gsung thugs kyi gsang chen gsang ba 'dus pa zhes bya ba brtag pa'i rgyal po chen po
P81, vol. 3; Toh. 442, vol. *ca;* Dharma vol. 29
Sanskrit text edited by S. Bagchi. *The Guhyasamāja Tantra.* Darbhanga, India: The Mithila Institute, 1965.

One Letter Perfection of Wisdom Sūtra
ekākṣarīmātānāmasarvatathāgataprajñāpāramitāsūtra
de bzhin gshegs pa thams cad kyi yum shes rab kyi pha rol tu phyin pa yi ge gcig ma'i mdo
P741, vol. 21; Toh. 23, Dharma vol. 12
English translation by Edward Conze. *The Short Prajñāpāramitā Texts,* p. 201. London: Luzac, 1973.

Purification of All Bad Transmigrations Tantra (partially concordant Yoga Tantra)
sarvadurgatipariśodhanatejorājasya tathāgatasya arhataḥ samyaksaṃbuddhasya kalpa
de bzhin gshegs pa dgra bcom pa yang dag par rdzogs pa'i sangs rgyas ngan song thams cad yong su sbyong ba gzi brjid kyi rgyal po'i rtog pa
P116, vol. 5; Toh. 483, vol. *ta*
Tibetan text and English translation: Tadeusz Skorupski. *The Sarvadurgatipariśodhana Tantra: Elimination of All Evil Destinies.* New Delhi: Motilal Banarsidass, 1983.

Purification of All Bad Transmigrations Tantra (partially concordant Yoga Tantra)
sarvadurgatipariśodhanatejorājasya tathāgatasya arhataḥ samyaksaṃbuddhasya kalpaikadeśa
de bzhin gshegs pa dgra bcom pa yang dag par rdzogs pa'i sangs rgyas ngan song thams cad yong su sbyong ba gzi brjid kyi rgyal po'i brtag pa phyogs gcig pa
P117, vol. 5; Toh. 485, vol. *ta*

Tibetan text and English translation: Tadeusz Skorupski. *The Sarvadurgatipariśodhana Tantra: Elimination of All Evil Destinies.* New Delhi: Motilal Banarsidass, 1983.

Sarvavid Vairochana Tantra

See *Purification of All Bad Transmigrations Tantra*

Shrīparamādya Tantra, Part One (partially concordant Yoga Tantra)

śrīparamādyanāmamahāyānakalparāja

dpal mchog dang po zhes bya ba theg pa chen po'i rtog pa'i rgyal po

P119, vol. 5; Toh. 487, vol. *ta*

Shrīparamādya Tantra, Part Two (partially concordant Yoga Tantra)

śrīparamādyamantrakalpakhaṇḍa

dpal mchog dang po'i sngags kyi rtog pa'i dum bu

P120, vol. 5; Toh. 488, vol. *ta*

Susiddhi Tantra (one of the four general Action Tantras)

susiddhikaramahātantrasādhanopāyikapaṭala

legs par grub par byed pa'i rgyud chen po las sgrub pa'i thabs rim par phye ba

P431, vol. 9; Toh. 807, Dharma vol. 34

Translation: Rolf W. Giebel. *Two Esoteric Sutras: The Adamantine Pinnacle Sutra; The Susiddhikara Sutra.* Berkeley, CA: Numata Center for Buddhist Translation and Research, 2001; *Adamantine Pinnacle Sutra* (= chapter 1 of *Tattvasaṅgraha*), 1-107; *Susiddhikara Sutra,* 109-325.

Vajrashekhara Tantra (explanatory tantra for the *Compendium of Principles Tantra*)

vajraśekharamahāguhyayogatantra

gsang ba rnal 'byor chen po'i rgyud rdo rje rtse mo

P113, vol. 5; Toh. 480, vol. *nya*

Vairochanābhisaṃbodhi (a Performance Tantra)

mahāvairocanābhisaṃbodhivikurvatī-adhiṣṭhānavaipūlyasūtra-indrarājanāmadharmaparyāya

rnam par snang mdzad chen po mngon par rdzogs par byang chub pa rnam par sprul ba byin gyis rlob pa shin tu rgyas pa mdo sde'i dbang po rgyal po zhes bya ba'i chos kyi rnam grangs

P126, vol. 5; Toh. 494, Dharma vol. 31

Translation: Stephen Hodge. *The Mahā-Vairocana-Abhisaṃbodhi Tantra with Buddhaguhya's Commentary.* London & New York: RoutledgeCurzon, 2003.

2. Other Sanskrit and Tibetan Works

Ānandagarbha (*kun dga' snying po;* tenth century)

Extensive Explanation of the "Shrīparamādya Tantra"

śrīparamādyaṭīkā

dpal mchog dang po'i rgya cher bshad pa

P3335, vols. 72-73; Toh. 2512, vols. *si-'i*

Illumination of the Principles: Explanation of the Tantra called "Compendium of the Principles of All Ones-Gone-Thus: Manifest Realization of the Great Vehicle"

sarvatathāgatatattvasaṁgrahamahāyānābhisamayatantratattvālokakārināmavyākhyā

de bzhin gshegs pa thams cad kyi de kho na nyid bsdus pa theg pa chen po mngon par rtogs pa zhes bya ba'i rgyud kyi bshad pa de kho na nyid snang bar byed pa

P3333, vols. 71-72; Toh. 2510, vol. *li*

Means of Achievement Called "Source of Vajrasattva" (the longer *Source of [Vajra]sattva* [*sems dpa' 'byung chen*])

vajrasattvodayanāmasādhana

rdo rje sems dpa' 'byung ba zhes bya ba'i sgrub pa'i thabs

P3340, vol. 74; Toh. 2517, Dharma vol. 57

Means of Achievement of Vajrasattva (the shorter *Source of [Vajra]sattva* [*sems dpa' 'byung chung*])

vajrasattvasādhana

rdo rje sems dpa'i sgrub pa'i thabs

P3341, vol. 74; Toh. 2518, Dharma vol. 57
Rite of the Vajra Element Great Maṇḍala: Source of All Vajras
vajradhātumahāmaṇḍalopāyikasarvavajrodaya
rdo rje dbyings kyi dkyil 'khor chen po'i cho ga rdo rje thams cad 'byung ba
P3339, vol. 74; Toh. 2516, vol. *ku*
Sanskrit: "Vajradhātumahāmaṇḍalopāyikā-Sarvavajrodayanāma—bonbun tekisuto to wayaku—(I)," *Annual of the Institute for Comprehensive Studies of Buddhism, Taisho University (Taishō Daigaku Sōgō Bukkyō Kunkyūjo nenpō)*, Issue 8 (1986), 258-224 and "Vajradhātumahāmaṇḍalopāyikā-Sarvavajrodayanāma—bonbun tekisuto to wayaku—(II)," *Annual of the Institute for Comprehensive Studies of Buddhism, Taisho University (Taishō Daigaku Sōgō Bukkyō Kunkyūjo nenpō)*, Issue 9 (1987), 294-222.
Asaṅga (*thogs med*, fourth century)
Explanation of (Maitreya's) "Sublime Continuum of the Great Vehicle"
mahāynottaratantraśāstravyākhya
theg pa chen po'i rgyud bla ma'i bstan bcos kyi rnam par bshad pa
P5526, vol. 108; Toh. 4025, Dharma vol. 77
Sanskrit: E. H. Johnston (and T. Chowdhury). *The Ratnagotravibhāga Mahāyānottaratantraśāstra.* Patna, India: Bihar Research Society, 1950.
English translation: E. Obermiller. "Sublime Science of the Great Vehicle to Salvation." *Acta Orientalia* 9 (1931): 81-306. Also: J. Takasaki. *A Study on the Ratnagotravibhāga.* Rome: Istituto Italiano per il Medio ed Estremo Oriente, 1966.
Five Treatises on the Grounds
1. *Grounds of Yogic Practice*
yogācārabhūmi
rnal 'byor spyod pa'i sa
P5536-5538, vols. 109-110; Toh. 4035-4037, Dharma vols. 78
Grounds of Bodhisattvas
bodhisattvabhūmi
byang chub sems pa'i sa
P5538, vol. 110; Toh. 4037, Dharma vol. 78
Sanskrit: Unrai Wogihara. *Bodhisattvabhūmi: A Statement of the Whole Course of the Bodhisattva (Being the Fifteenth Section of Yogācārabhūmi).* Leipzig: 1908; Tokyo: Seigo Kenyūkai, 1930-1936. Also: Nalinaksha Dutt. *Bodhisattvabhumi (Being the XVth Section of Asangapada's Yogacarabhumi).* Tibetan Sanskrit Works Series, 7. Patna, India: K. P. Jayaswal Research Institute, 1966.
English translation of the Chapter on Suchness, the fourth chapter of Part I, which is the fifteenth volume of the *Grounds of Yogic Practice:* Janice D. Willis. *On Knowing Reality.* New York: Columbia University Press, 1979; reprint, Delhi: Motilal Banarsidass, 1979.
2. *Compendium of Ascertainments*
nirṇayasaṃgraha / viniścayasaṃgrahaṇī
rnam par gtan la dbab pa bsdu ba
P5539, vols. 110-111, Toh. 4038, vol. *zi*
3. *Compendium of Bases*
vastusaṃgraha
gzhi bsdu ba
P5540, vol. 111; Toh. 4039, Dharma vol. 79
4. *Compendium of Enumerations*
paryāyasaṃgraha
rnam grang bsdu ba
P5542, vol. 111; Toh. 4041, Dharma vol. 79
5. *Compendium of Explanations*
vivaraṇasaṃgraha
rnam par bshad pa bsdu ba

P5543, vol. 111; Toh. 4042, Dharma vol. 79

Bhāvaviveka (*legs ldan 'byed,* c. 500-570?)

Heart of the Middle

madhyamakahṛdaya

dbu ma'i snying po

P5255, vol. 96; Toh. 3855, vol. *dza*

Bu-dön (*bu ston,* 1290-1364)

Condensed General Presentation of the Tantra Sets: Key Opening the Door to the Precious Treasury of Tantra Sets

rgyud sde spyi'i rnam gzhag bsdus pa / rgyud sde spyi'i rnam par gzhag pa rgyud sde rin po che'i gter sgo 'byed pa'i lde mig

Collected Works, vol. 14, 843.1-1013.3. Śata Piṭaka No. 54. New Delhi: International Academy of Indian Culture, 1969; Toh. 5167.

Extensive Explanation of (Ānandagarbha's) "Source of All Vajras": Wish-Granting Jewel

rdo rje thams cad 'byung ba'i rgya cher bshad pa yid bzhin nor bu

Collected Works, vol. 11, 185-832. Śata Piṭaka No. 51. New Delhi: International Academy of Indian Culture, 1968.

Extensive General Presentation of the Tantra Sets: Ornament Beautifying the Precious Tantra Sets

rgyud sde spyi rnam rgyas pa / rgyud sde spyi'i rnam par gzhag pa rgyud sde rin po che'i mdzes rgyan

Collected Works, vol. 15, 1.1-609.7. Śata Piṭaka No. 55. New Delhi: International Academy of Indian Culture, 1969; Toh. 5169.

Medium Length General Presentation of the Tantra Sets: Illuminating the Secrets of All Tantra Sets

rgyud sde spyi rnam 'bring po / rgyud sde spyi'i rnam par gzhag pa rgyud sde thams cad kyi gsang ba gsal bar byed pa

Collected Works, vol. 15, 611.1-913.7. Śata Piṭaka No. 55. New Delhi: International Academy of Indian Culture, 1969; Toh. 5168.

Practice of (Ānandagarbha's) "Rite of the Vajra Element [Great] Maṇḍala: Source of All Vajras": Wish-Fulfilling Gem[a]

rdo rje dbyings kyi dkyil 'khor gyi cho ga rdo rje thams cad 'byung ba zhes bya ba'i lag len rin chen bsam 'phel

Collected Works, vol. 12, 169-326. Śata Piṭaka No. 52. New Delhi: International Academy of Indian Culture, 1968.

Ship for Launching onto the Ocean of Yoga Tantra

rnal 'byor rgyud gyi rgya mtshor 'jug pa'i gru gzings

Collected Works, vol. 11. Śata Piṭaka No. 51. New Delhi: International Academy of Indian Culture, 1968.

Buddhaguhya (*sangs rgyas gsang ba*)

Commentary on the "Vairochanābhisambodhi Tantra" / Explanation of the "Vairochanābhisambodhi Tantra"

vairocanābhisambodhivikurvitādhiṣṭhānamahātantravṛtti

rnam par snang mdzad mngon par byang chub pa rnam par sprul pa'i byin gyis brlabs kyi rgyud chen po'i 'grel pa

P3490, vol.77, p. 229, *rgyud 'grel, cu* 1-230a.5; D2663, *rgyud, nyu* 261a.1-*tu* 116a.7;

Also: vairocanābhisambodhivikurvitādhiṣṭhānamahātantrabhāṣya

rnam par snang mdzad mngon par byang chub pa rnam par sprul pa'i byin gyis brlabs kyi rgyud chen po'i bshad pa

P3487, vol.77, p. 110, *rgyud 'grel, ngu* 76b.8-337a.3; D2663, *rgyud, nyu* 65a.3-260b.7.

Translation of Chapters 1 and 2: Alex Wayman and R. Tajima. *The Enlightenment of Vairocana.*

---

[a] This is Bu-dön's Tibetanization of the translation of Ānandagarbha's text; see the previous entry for his full-fledged commentary.

Delhi: Motilal Banarsidass, 1992.
Translation: Stephen Hodge. *The Mahā-Vairocana-Abhisaṃbodhi Tantra with Buddhaguhya's Commentary.* London & New York: RoutledgeCurzon, 2003.
Condensation of the "Vairochanābhisambodhi Tantra"
vairocanābhisambodhitantrapiṇḍārtha
rnam par snang mdzad mngon par rdzogs par byang chub pa'i rgyud kyi bsdus pa'i don
P3486, vol. 77
Translation: Stephen Hodge. *The Mahā-Vairocana-Abhisaṃbodhi Tantra with Buddhaguhya's Commentary.* London & New York: RoutledgeCurzon, 2003.
Introducing the Meaning of the [Compendium of Principles] Tantra
tantrārthāvatāra
rgyud kyi don la 'jug pa
P3324, vol. 70; Toh. 2501, vol. *'i.*

Chandrakīrti (*zla ba grags pa,* seventh century)
Supplement to (Nāgārjuna's) "Treatise on the Middle"
madhyamakāvatāra
dbu ma la 'jug pa
P5262, vol. 98; Toh. 3861, vol. *'a*
Tibetan: Louis de La Vallée Poussin. *Madhyamakāvatāra par Candrakīrti.* Bibliotheca Buddhica, 9. Osnabrück, Germany: Biblio Verlag, 1970.
English translation (chap. 1-5): Jeffrey Hopkins. *Compassion in Tibetan Buddhism.* London: Rider, 1980; reprint, Ithaca, N.Y.: Snow Lion, 1980.
English translation (chap. 6): Stephen Batchelor. *Echoes of Voidness* by Geshé Rabten, 47-92. London: Wisdom, 1983.
English translation: C. W. Huntington, Jr. *The Emptiness of Emptiness: An Introduction to Early Indian Mādhyamika,* 147-195. Honolulu, Hawaii: University of Hawaii Press, 1989.
French translation (up to chap. 6, stanza 165): Louis de La Vallée Poussin. *Muséon* 8 (1907): 249-317; *Muséon* 11 (1910): 271-358; *Muséon* 12 (1911): 235-328.
German translation (chap. 6, 166-226): Helmut Tauscher. *Candrakīrti-Madhyamakāvatāraḥ und Madhyamakāvatārabhāṣyam.* Vienna: Wiener Studien zur Tibetologie und Buddhismuskunde, 1981.

Ḏzong-ka-ḇa Ḻo-sang-drak-ḇa (*tsong kha pa blo bzang grags pa,* 1357-1419)
Explanation of the Root Infractions
rtsa ltung gi rnam bshad / gsang sngags kyi tshul khrims kyi rnam bshad dngos grub kyi snye ma
P6188, vol. 160
English translation: Gareth Sparham. *Tantric Ethics: An Explanation of the Precepts for Buddhist Vajrayāna Practice.* Boston: Wisdom, 2005.
Great Exposition of Secret Mantra / The Stages of the Path to a Conqueror and Pervasive Master, a Great Vajradhara: Revealing All Secret Topics
rgyal ba khyab bdag rdo rje 'chang chen po'i lam gyi rim pa gsang ba kun gyi gnad rnam par phye ba
P6210, vol. 161. Also: Dharmsala, India: Shes rig par khang, 1969. Also: The Collected Works of Rje Tsoṅ-kha-pa Blo-bzaṅ-grags-pa (Reproduced from an example of the old Bkra-sis-lhun-po redaction from the library of Klu 'khyil Monastery of Ladakh), vols. 4 and 5. New Delhi: Ngawang Gelek, 1975. Also: The Collected Works (gsuṅ 'bum) of the Incomparable Lord Tsoṅ-kha-pa Blo-bzaṅ-grags-pa (Reproduced from prints from the 1897 Lha-sa Old Zhol [Dga'-ldan-phun-tshogs-gliṅ] blocks), vol. 3. New Delhi: Guru Deva, 1978-1979.
English translation (Chapter 1): H.H. the Dalai Lama, Tsong-ka-pa, and Jeffrey Hopkins. *Tantra in Tibet.* London: George Allen and Unwin, 1977; reprint, with minor corrections, Ithaca, N.Y.: Snow Lion, 1987.
English translation (Chapters 2 and 3): H.H. the Dalai Lama, Tsong-ka-pa, and Jeffrey Hopkins. *The Yoga of Tibet.* London: George Allen and Unwin, 1981; reprinted as *Deity Yoga.* Ithaca, N.Y.: Snow Lion, 1987.

English translation (Chapter 4) in this book.

Japanese translation (Chapters 1-4): Ninkaku Takata. *A Study of Indo-Tibetan Mantrayāna Buddhism.* Koyasan: Mikkyo Gakujutsu Shinkokai, 1978.

Great Exposition of the Stages of the Path / Stages of the Path to Enlightenment Thoroughly Teaching All the Stages of Practice of the Three Types of Beings

lam rim chen mo / skyes bu gsum gyi nyams su blang ba'i rim pa thams cad tshang bar ston pa'i byang chub lam gyi rim pa

P6001, vol. 152. Also: Dharmsala, India: Tibetan Cultural Printing Press, 1964. Also: The Collected Works of Rje Tsoṅ-kha-pa Blo-bzaṅ-grags-pa (Reproduced from an example of the old Bkra-sis-lhun-po redaction from the library of Klu 'khyil Monastery of Ladakh), vols. 19 and 20. New Delhi: Ngawang Gelek, 1975. Also: The Collected Works (gsuṅ 'bum) of the Incomparable Lord Tsoṅ-kha-pa Blo-bzaṅ-grags-pa (Reproduced from prints from the 1897 Lha-sa Old Zhol [Dga'-ldan-phun-tshogs-gliṅ] blocks), vol. 13. New Delhi: Guru Deva, 1978-1979.

English translation: Lamrim Chenmo Translation Committee. *The Great Treatise on the Stages of the Path to Enlightenment.* Joshua W.C. Cutler, editor-in-chief, Guy Newland, editor. 3 vols. Ithaca, N.Y.: Snow Lion, 2000-2004.

English translation of the part on the excessively broad object of negation: Elizabeth Napper. *Dependent-Arising and Emptiness,* 153-215. London: Wisdom, 1989.

English translation of the part on the excessively narrow object of negation: William Magee. *The Nature of Things: Emptiness and Essence in the Geluk World,* 179-192. Ithaca, New York: Snow Lion, 1999.

English translation of the parts on calm abiding and special insight: Alex Wayman. *Calming the Mind and Discerning the Real,* 81-431. New York: Columbia University Press, 1978; reprint, New Delhi, Motilal Banarsidass, 1979.

Medium Exposition of the Stages of the Path / Small Exposition of the Stages of the Path to Enlightenment

lam rim 'bring / lam rim chung ngu / skyes bu gsum gyi nyams su blang ba'i byang chub lam gyi rim pa

P6002, vol. 152-153. Also: Dharmsala, India: Tibetan Cultural Printing Press, 1968. Also: Mundgod, India: dga' ldan shar rtse, n.d. (includes outline of topics by Trijang Rinbochay). Also: The Collected Works of Rje Tsoṅ-kha-pa Blo-bzaṅ-grags-pa (Reproduced from an example of the old Bkra-sis-lhun-po redaction from the library of Klu 'khyil Monastery of Ladakh), vol. 21, 1-438. New Delhi: Ngawang Gelek, 1975. Also: The Collected Works (gsuṅ 'bum) of the Incomparable Lord Tsoṅ-kha-pa Blo-bzaṅ-grags-pa (Reproduced from prints from the 1897 Lha-sa Old Zhol [Dga'-ldan-phun-tshogs-gliṅ] blocks), vol. 14. New Delhi: Guru Deva, 1978-1979.

English translation of the section on special insight: Jeffrey Hopkins. *Other-Emptiness Self-Emptiness: Döl-b̄o-b̄a and D̄zong-ka-b̄a.* Ithaca, N.Y.: Snow Lion Publications, forthcoming. Also, Robert Thurman. "The Middle Transcendent Insight." *Life and Teachings of Tsong Khapa,* 108-185. Dharmsala, India: Library of Tibetan Works and Archives, 1982.

"Purification of All Bad Transmigrations Tantra" with Annotations from the Speech of the Foremost [D̄zong-ka-b̄a], Written by Gyel-d̄eng-ba Dön-drup-b̄el

ngan song sbyong ba'i rgyud rje'i gsung gi mchan dang bcas pa, *written down by* rgyal stengs pa don grub dpal

The Collected Works of rJe Tsoṅ-kha-pa blo-bzaṅ-grags-pa, vol. 15. New Delhi: Ngawang Gelek Demo, 1975.

Kamalashīla (c.740-795)

Stages of Meditation

bhāvanākrama

sgom pa'i rim pa

P5310-5312, vol. 102; Toh. 3915-3917, Dharma vol. 73, Tokyo *sde dge* vol. 15

Sanskrit: *First Bhāvanākrama.* G. Tucci, ed. *Minor Buddhist texts, II,* Serie Orientale Roma IX, 2. Rome: Is.M.E.O., 1958, pp. 185-229. *Third Bhāvanākrama.* G. Tucci, ed. *Minor Buddhist texts, III,* Serie Orientale Roma XLIII. Rome: Is.M.E.O., 1971.

Tibetan and English: *Second Bhāvanākrama.* The Dalai Lama. *Stages of Meditation.* Translated by Venerable Geshe Lobsang Jordhen, Losang Choephel Ganchenpa, and Jeremy Russell. Ithaca, N.Y.: Snow Lion Publications, 2001.

Ke-drup Ge-lek-b̄el-sang (*mkhas grub dge legs dpal bzang,* 1385-1438)

Extensive Explanation of the Format of the General Tantra Sets

rgyud sde spyi'i rnam par bzhag pa rgyas par bshad pa

Collected Works of the Lord Mkhas-grub rje dge-legs-dpal-bzaṅ-po, vol. 8, 443-630. New Delhi: Guru Deva, 1980. Also: Collected Works of Mkhas-grub dge-legs dpal, vol. 11, 215-368. New Delhi: Ngawang Gelek Demo, 1983.

Edited and translated by Ferdinand D. Lessing and Alex Wayman. *Mkhas Grub Rje's Fundamentals of the Buddhist Tantras.* The Hague: Mouton, 1968; reprint, Delhi: Motilal Banarsidass, 1978.

Lo-sang-chö-ḡyi-gyel-tsen (*blo bzang chos kyi rgyal mtshan,* 1567[?]-1662)

Notes on a Presentation of the General Teaching and the Tantra Sets

bstan pa spyi dang rgyud sde bzhi'i rnam par bzhag pa'i zin bris

Collected Works, vol. 4.New Delhi: Gurudeva, 1973.

Maitreya (*byams pa*)

Five Doctrines of Maitreya

1. *Great Vehicle Treatise on the Sublime Continuum*

mahāyānottaratantraśāstra

theg pa chen po rgyud bla ma'i bstan bcos

P5525, vol. 108; Toh. 4024, Dharma vol. 77

Sanskrit: E. H. Johnston (and T. Chowdhury). *The Ratnagotravibhāga Mahāyānottaratantraśāstra.* Patna, India: Bihar Research Society, 1950.

English translation: E. Obermiller. "Sublime Science of the Great Vehicle to Salvation." *Acta Orientalia* 9 (1931): 81-306. Also: J. Takasaki. *A Study on the Ratnagotravibhāga.* Rome: Istituto Italiano per il Medio ed Estremo Oriente, 1966.

2. *Differentiation of Phenomena and the Final Nature of Phenomena*

dharmadharmatāvibhaṅga

chos dang chos nyid rnam par 'byed pa

P5523, vol. 108; Toh. 4022, Dharma vol. 77

English translation: Jim Scott. *Maitreya's Distinguishing Phenomena and Pure Being with commentary by Mipham.* Ithaca, New York: Snow Lion, 2004.

3. *Differentiation of the Middle and the Extremes*

madhyāntavibhaṅga

dbus dang mtha' rnam par 'byed pa

P5522, vol. 108; Toh. 4021, Dharma vol. 77

Sanskrit: Gadjin M. Nagao. *Madhyāntavibhāga-bhāṣya.* Tokyo: Suzuki Research Foundation, 1964. Also: Ramchandra Pandeya. *Madhyānta-vibhāga-śāstra.* Delhi: Motilal Banarsidass, 1971.

English translation: Stefan Anacker. *Seven Works of Vasubandhu.* Delhi: Motilal Banarsidass, 1984. Also, of chapter 1: Thomas A. Kochumuttom. *A Buddhist Doctrine of Experience.* Delhi: Motilal Banarsidass, 1982. Also, of chapter 1: F. Th. Stcherbatsky. *Madhyāntavibhāga, Discourse on Discrimination between Middle and Extremes Ascribed to Bodhisattva Maitreya and Commented by Vasubandhu and Sthiramati.* Bibliotheca Buddhica, 30 (1936). Osnabrück, Germany: Biblio Verlag, 1970; reprint, Calcutta: Indian Studies Past and Present, 1971. Also, of chapter 1: David Lasar Friedmann. *Sthiramati, Madhyāntavibhāgaṭīkā: Analysis of the Middle Path and the Extremes.* Utrecht, Netherlands: Rijksuniversiteit te Leiden, 1937.

4. *Ornament for Clear Realization*

abhisamayālaṃkāra-prajñāpāramitopadeśaśāstra

shes rab kyi pha rol tu phyin pa'i man ngag gi bstan bcos mngon par rtogs pa'i rgyan

P5184, vol. 88; Toh. 3786, Dharma vol. 63

Sanskrit: Th. Stcherbatsky and E. Obermiller, eds. *Abhisamayālaṃkāra-Prajñāpāramitā-Upadeśa-Śāstra.* Bibliotheca Buddhica, 23. Osnabrück, Germany: Biblio Verlag, 1970.

English translation: Edward Conze. *Abhisamayālaṃkāra.* Serie Orientale Rome. Rome: Istituto

Italiano per il Medio ed Estremo Oriente, 1954.
5. *Ornament for the Great Vehicle Sūtras*
mahāyānasūtrālaṃkāra
theg pa chen po'i mdo sde rgyan gyi tshig le'ur byas pa
P5521, vol. 108; Toh. 4020, Dharma vol. 77
Sanskrit: Sitansusekhar Bagchi. *Mahāyāna-Sūtrālaṃkāraḥ of Asaṅga* [with Vasubandhu's commentary]. Buddhist Sanskrit Texts, 13. Darbhanga, India: Mithila Institute, 1970.
Sanskrit text and translation into French: Sylvain Lévi. *Mahāyānasūtrālaṃkāra, exposé de la doctrine du grand véhicule selon le système Yogācāra.* 2 vols. Paris: Bibliothèque de l'École des Hautes Études, 1907, 1911.
Sanskrit text and translation into English: Surekha Vijay Limaye. *Mahāyānasūtrālaṃkāra by Asaṅga.* Bibliotheca Indo-Buddhica Series, 94. Delhi: Sri Satguru, 1992.
English translation: L. Jamspal. *The Universal Vehicles Discourse Literature.* Editor-in-chief, Robert A.F Thurman. New York: American Institute of Buddhist Studies, Columbia University, 2004

Padmavajra (*skal bzang rdo rje*)
Commentarial Explanation of (Buddhaguhya's) "Introduction to the Meaning of the Tantra"
tantrārthāvatāravyākhyāna
rgyud kyi don la 'jug pa'i 'grel bshad
P3325, vol. 70; Toh. 2502, vol. *'i.*

Paṇ-chen Sö-nam-drak-b̄a (*paṇ chen bsod nams grags pa,* 1478-1554)
General Presentation of the Tantra Sets: Captivating the Minds of the Fortunate
rgyud sde spyi'i rnam par bzhag pa skal bzang gi yid 'phrog
Dharamsala, Library of Tibetan Works and Archives, 1975

Ratnākarashānti (*ratnākaraśānti, rin chen 'byung gnas zhi ba*)
Quintessential Instructions on the Perfection of Wisdom
prajñāpāramitopadeśa
shes rab kyi pha rol tu phyin pa'i man ngag
P5798, vol. 114; Toh. 4079, Dharma vol. 81

Shākyamitra (*shākya'i bshes gnyen*)
Ornament of Kosala
kosalālaṃkāratattvasaṃgrahaṭīkā
de kho na nyid bsdus pa'i rgya cher bshad pa ko sa la'i rgyan
P3326, vols. 70-71; Toh. 2503, vol. *yi.*

Index